No Experience Necessary:

An Uncanny Small Business Survival Guide

Tim Kissman

AmErica House
Baltimore

© 2001 by Tim Kissman.

First printing

ISBN: 1-58851-686-5
PUBLISHED BY AMERICA HOUSE BOOK
PUBLISHERS
www.publishamerica.com
Baltimore

Printed in the United States of America

To my family.

I'd like to thank the Small Business Association of Michigan, its board of directors and staff, for assisting me in this endeavor. Without the countless hours small business owners spend at their careers, and the success that follows with hard work, this book would have never been possible.

Table of contents

Introduction: What is *No Experience Necessary*

Part One: General Business Tips

Part Two: Manners and First Impressions

Part Five: Human Resources and How to Stretch the Dollar

Part Six: Marketing

Part Seven: 'Tis the Seasonal Tips and Keeping Stress to a Minimum

Appendix: What is the Small Business Association of Michigan?

Introduction

I can't wear hats.

Hat companies simply don't make them large enough to fit my head. So when I attend small business conferences and mingle with small entrepreneurs, I don't participate in conversations when they speak about how different hats are important for success. If I did I'd be lying.

Sure, I've tried to make a hat fit. I've ripped out the inside, stretched it and made little notches along the seams, but nothing works. The only hats that fit are winter hats or golf visors, but those aren't the same. I have plenty of experiences to share as the owner of my own Web design and creative writing business, Limelight Creations, but without a hat how can I contribute?

Instead of talking, I listened. Every small business owner in the world is eager to share how to make a business work and what he or she is doing to take it to the next level. I take notes on how they cope with unruly employees, rising taxes or stubborn vendors. I observe how they're dressed, how they behave and how they talk. By the end of those meetings, I come away with more tips than I could possibly use in my one-person, home-based venture.

That's why I started writing my column "No Experience Necessary" for the Small Business Association of Michigan. It's designed to give small business owners, or future entrepreneurs, tips and ideas to make their business better. I try to make the advice witty and light because running a business is tough. It's nice to laugh once in a while and know you're not alone in your endeavor. Others have jumped through the same hoops.

Through the years I've interviewed hundreds of small business owners, each with advice on how to make it to the top. These people inspire me to continue to write my column and make my company succeed. There have been plenty of tips and experiences to go around. I've also created some interesting small business characters along the way to help illustrate my point. They can be a bit unruly at times.

Yeah, put a plug in for me, Tim. E-mail Eddie, your e-mail buddy.

I just did, E-mail Eddie.

Sorry about that. He's eager to start.

E-mail Eddie is always eager to help a small business owner.

Bye, Eddie.

Bye.

As I stitch bathroom cleaner and carpenter patches to my winter hats while lawn mower and window washer are taped to my golf visor, I know that owning a small business is a challenge.

But if, and when, you succeed, you won't even feel the pressure of all those hats on your head anymore because you'll be floating in the clouds with a successful business. What a feeling. Unless of course, you're like me and the hat cuts the blood circulation to your brain.

Then you'll just be unconscious. Happy, but out cold.

Part One:
General Office Tips

    This section helps small business owners select office plants, learn why the paper clip is one of the best office items ever invented and whether to use blue or black ink when writing business correspondence. There are so many things to consider when running a business. Who has the time to think about the trivial items? That answer is easy: me!

Turn down the radio, turn up the creativity

Inspiration takes many forms.

People look at paintings, read motivational sayings, see an adrenaline charged movie or immerse themselves in solitude to bring out their creative side. I think all those are grand, but not for the workplace.

My biggest inspiration, relaxation, motivation and any other word you can put -ion at the end of, is music. It's a great way to relax and with a creative job like mine, it can put me on the road to a great story.

This method is a popular for employees, but also opens the door to potential problems. What happens when music conflicts and causes a disturbance? What happens when several radios, in an open workspace, are on at the same time?

One day, when I ran smack dab into writer's block, I turned up my radio to get the creative juices flowing. While Steppenwolf told me they were "Born to be Wild," I put my head down to think.

A co-worker farther down in my row of desks must have had the same writer's block because they turned their radio on. Jimmy Buffet was their cure, though. I like Buffet, but I wanted Steppenwolf. I inched my volume control up. That lasted for about three seconds before Jimmy sang out, louder than ever, that he was looking for his lost shaker of salt.

When the music becomes a disruption and work suffers, it hurts office morale. Telling employees to shut their radio off does the same and it may make creativity suffer.

These are two things no small business owner wants to deal

with during the course of a day.

Here are some ideas to tune out the distraction and tune in better work:

Head it off. Headphones are the simplest cure. Ask employees to plug in a set of headphones and keep working. Hold back the volume, too. Take note, though, this solution doesn't work in a public office setting.

Same station, different day. Reach a compromise and play only one radio a week. Choose a particular station for each day. Monday can be easy listening, Tuesday country, etc. That way everyone is happy at least one day of the week.

Floor it. If it's in an open office, block the sound from traveling by putting the radio on the floor next to a desk. It creates a great buffer.

Small business employees have a unique situation because, for the most part, they work in a small, close-knit environment. It's important to nurture creativity. It just takes a little consideration to make music problems disappear.

Tim has left the building.

Small business employees may have to wear more than one hat

As the owner of a small business, being a jack of all trades isn't an option. Every office job, from emptying wastebaskets to fixing the copy machine, becomes part of the job.

As the employee of a small business, however, the idea of wearing a multitude of hats doesn't sit well sometimes. Usually hired for a single purpose, the average employee doesn't venture into the many different tasks that make an office run smoothly.

I ran into this problem when I managed a small newspaper. No one wanted to clean the bathroom. We couldn't agree on a suitable system. Of all places to face an impasse, the bathroom was not a good one. Garbage overflowed from the trash can and the floor never looked clean. Bathroom supplies were as precious as gold and never in abundance.

The system we set up to give everyone responsibility didn't work. The scheduled employee may have been busy and couldn't clean it, leaving the next scheduled person with the dirty deed.

We looked into paying someone, but it didn't fit the budget. Besides, it shouldn't have been a major problem and we felt we could get it done. I eventually met with my boss and decided we would split the task. After that day, we came up with some ideas to avoid problems in the future:

Start early. Come up with a policy. Tell employees they'll have to clean when asked. If that doesn't work, change the job description. If that still doesn't work, replace the employee.

Contest the thought. My parents gave me extra incentive to do my chores by promising an allowance. Who says this doesn't have to apply to the work place? If the employees keep their workstation neat and pitch in around the office, reward them with lunch or an office party.

Common threads. When it comes to a common area like the kitchen or restroom you may not be able to convince your employees to clean. Try this instead: Tell them you'll take the bathroom if they'll run the mail to the post office or clean the kitchen. I know I'd be a familiar face at the post office in a hurry given that choice.

The bathroom problem went away. We still had to deal with that green thing that lived in the refrigerator for more than a year, though.

We decided to take out life insurance before tackling that problem.

Thinking about starting your own business? Make sure you do the research

At one time or another we've all worked for a boss we'd like to forget. My experience came with dismal office space, weekly tantrums and an employee policy manual I swear the devil wrote.

There were only four employees and we talked quite a bit about our options in case of a mass firing. It seemed everybody had an alternative plan. Our sales person said she could begin work at a rival magazine with one phone call. Our senior writer said she had a job lined up out-of-state that was perfect for her. An editor said he would work at his father's business.

That left me. I had no plan, no option and I was getting nervous. I looked into running my own business. I was sick of dealing with a boss I didn't like and the idea of never taking another order sounded delicious.

It was time to explore my options before anything happened. I wanted to start my own magazine — a dream I've had for some time and one that is still there.

I spent several weeks doing research. I thought just having deep enough pockets and a thorough business plan would be enough to launch a business, but I was wrong.

There's much more to it than meets the eye.

Here's what I found:

Play the organ-izations. There are plenty of statewide organizations that exist to help businesses get off the ground. The Small Business Association of Michigan is a great place to start. Also, the Michigan Small Business Development Centers at your local universities are another terrific resource. The government's Small Business Administration also has great information available. Visit SBAM's Web site at *www.sbam.org* to find out more.

Are you seeing yellow? The phone book is a good place to see if your business idea can fly. See how many other businesses like the one you want to create exist. It's a measuring stick for competition and may give you advertising ideas.

Look in the library. Read everything you can about successful businesses. The library is an excellent source to learn about small businesses that made it big. Everybody started out small at one point. Find out how they made it big and see if your idea can fit into that mold.

Use your down time wisely, it doesn't come often

There may be a time in a small business owner's life when there is nothing to do. I know it seems improbable, maybe even too fantastic to believe, but it happens

It's a fleeting moment in time, much like the flash from a camera or a blink of an eye. I've been in this situation before. I remember it distinctly. Five years ago, a Tuesday, my work was completed, the desktop was clean, what should I do to pass the time? It was then I saw them for the first time. A little guy in a white business suit appeared on one shoulder; another little guy in a red business suit appeared on the other. He was a snappy dresser.

The red suit spoke up.

"Surf the Internet and find some online games. You can beat the high score from that teenager who just got home from school. You know the Web site address," he said. "That'll keep you busy for a while. No one will know you're playing."

"Spend the time learning a new computer application. No one's perfect and we all need to fine-tune our skills," the white suit replied. "I know you have some plans for a new newsletter. Design it on the computer. Imagine how much money you could save with in-house productions."

The little guy in the red suit poked me with his briefcase. It was pretty sharp.

"Hey, here's an idea," he said. "Take an extra-long lunch. Treat yourself to a juicy steak. You deserve it, look how hard you work."

"If you need a break, why not take a walk on the outside of your building and pick up trash, sweep the front steps or clean an area that you put off for other projects?" the white suit said. "Down time is precious and if you need some physical labor, do it for your business."

I cracked my neck and accidentally knocked the red-suited guy off my shoulder. He climbed back on and went right into my ear and started to whisper.

"The golf course, Tim," he said softly. "It's that time of year. Your clubs are in the garage. Go get them and play. You deserve it. Think of all those summer days you couldn't make it to the course like those other small business owners. Break free and play."

The little white-suited guy shook his head.

"He's losing his touch," he laughed. "It's February. There's snow on the ground. Use the time to better yourself. Help an employee with a project, clean your desk, reorganize your files, get all of your expense receipts in order; there are a million things you could do. Success comes to those who earn it."

The white-suited guy was right. I knew it and nodded. The minute I did, both figures disappeared. I couldn't believe it, my first time with nothing pressing to do and I get a visit from figments of my imagination.

I guess it pays to be busy.

Now my files are in immaculate order, as is the rest of my desk.

The little white-suited guy was right.

Golf still would be nice, but that can wait for the weekend…
… and summer.

Let this idea grow in your head: Plants are important office tools

My office plants don't like me.

I have them because it makes the room feel cozy and they look nice. But they've been giving me the droopy leaves bit and I'm starting to take it personally.

At one time my office had bare walls. The tall green plant and its short buddy were all the decoration I had. When people came into my office they could either look at the plants or look at me. As luck would have it, the plants received all the attention.

I was green with envy. They were happy, though. With bright leaves they loved being the focal point. That was fine by me, but it eventually turned out to be the root of a much bigger problem.

I bought some art for my walls and made the office a bit more interesting. My sports-themed posters and portraits have now become a conversation piece. That's when trouble sprouted.

The healthy plants turned ugly. They dropped leaves, turned brown and at one time, even housed bugs. My green thumb turned blue and I had to find ways to make sure they stayed alive. Luckily, I found some great tips and saved the plants. They worked for me and I'm sure these will grow on you, too:

Light it up. It's important to keep plants in a naturally lighted area. It doesn't matter how many lights you have in the office; it won't help the plant as much as the sun. The better the sunlight, the longer the plant will live. There are plants that do better in shaded areas than in lighted ones, so it helps to ask questions when making a purchase.

Pot luck. Make sure you have the right-sized pot for your plant. If the roots begin sticking out, it's time to replant. The roots need a place to grow and don't over water the pot. Over-watering and under-watering are the biggest villains in a plant's demise.

Avoid the extremes. Keep the plants at room temperature and don't expose them to severe temperature changes. If it's too cold or hot, they won't survive.

It's a good thing I found this advice. Otherwise, I was ready to name the plants and start singing to them, too. Anything to keep those guys alive.

Everyone in my office is grateful it didn't come to that.

Getting past the writer's block: Try this at home

It's easy to gauge the flow of creativity in my office. Just stand about 10 feet away from my door and listen.

If you can hear me typing on my keyboard I'm in a groove and making great headway. If you can't hear anything, take a closer look and you'll probably see a rabid case of writer's block. I've stared blankly at the screen for hours, chewed on pens until ink explodes on my face, and whispered conversations with myself.

"Tim, you're not doing too well today."

"Well, thanks Tim. I know that. You're not doing too well, either."

"If you would stop talking maybe I could concentrate."

"I was thinking the same thing about you."

"Well fine, then. Stare at the screen, see if I care."

"Maybe I will. Take that pen out of your mouth so I can understand you."

"Screen-starer!"

"Pen-chewer!"

You get the drift.

Every writer goes through it at one time or another so if you're a small business owner, trying his or her hand as a wordsmith, don't get frustrated.

Here are some methods I use to get past the blockage:

Change gears. Try something else, preferably something that requires physical activity. Sometimes thinking about a project too hard can bog you down. This excuse never worked in grade school, but there is some truth to it in the business world.

Chatter. Go talk to someone about the problem. You never know where you can find help, so don't be afraid to talk to the first person you see.

Write on. One of the most effective methods I use to get through a block is to keep writing. No matter how bad it sounds or how many different times I write one word over and over again, I keep plugging away. Usually I get to a point where I can't take it anymore and get mad enough to get over the hump. Then the words flow.

Make sure no one is in the room when you start talking to yourself. Having a writing block is a bad enough problem by itself. Having people stare at you while you scream yourself into a frenzy isn't that good of an idea.

My top 10 list of all-office items

Here's my top 10 list of all- office items that have made the small businessperson's life easier.

10. **The coffee mug.** My favorite one is Dan Marino, future Hall of Fame Miami Dolphins quarterback. Who can get any work done without a cup of java in the morning? Come to think

of it, I'm kind of tired right now, let me finish this cup and I'll tell you.

9. The radio. If there's a better way to have background noise, I've yet to find it. The radio is a must have for an office. At my home office, it's the television. That's a little dangerous though because it's hard to write and watch weekend football at the same time. Thank goodness I know home row.

8. The business card. Before day planners or personal data assistants, the business card reigned. Fresh with your own design, these little pieces of paper have helped seal more deals than Monty Hall. Some people are better at passing them out than others. I've been at my current job for three years now and still have my original box. Anyone interested in one?

7. A paper clip. Why one, you ask? Not only is that one paper clip strong enough to hold a dozen pieces of paper together, but it's also a great time killer. You can bend a paper clip into a million different shapes, break it into a million different pieces and fling it pretty far with a rubber band.

6. A nice desk. For those small business owners (like me) who struggle at the kitchen table, a makeshift board balanced haphazardly on a stack of cinder blocks or the hard wood floor, this one's for you. You never really appreciate what a nice desk can do for your productivity until you have one. Just keep it clean. Now where did I put my notes?

5. A break. That's right, a break. It can be five minutes, or a lunch, but where would we be without a little time to ourselves? I could name any number of times during the day when I could have performed much better with a little stress relief. But I won't do that now; it's almost lunchtime. I'll do it when I get back.

4. Snappy clothes. Dressing up may be a nuisance, especially for those co-workers who don't know the meaning of dress code, but for others it makes a difference. By taking pride in your appearance, you send a positive message. Like I told my freshman high school girl's basketball team: You look good, you feel good. They finished 1-17, but looked good going to games.

3. **The phone.** A lot of small business people would disagree with this one, saying it's more of a nuisance than an all-office selection, but I beg to differ. When people track you down, they want to talk business — even at home, when you're eating dinner with your family after a hard day's work. That brings me to 3a: Caller I.D.

2. **Pencils.** Ironic placement, isn't it?

1. **The computer.** In my case it's a Macintosh, for others it's a PC. E-mails, Web sites, e-commerce and any other type of business that begins with "e" has revolutionized business and made a lot of people really rich.

If only I could only be rich, too.

Find out what your competitor is up to before it's too late

Slick. That's how I describe the methods our chief competitor used to spy on my gig. It was cloak and dagger, James Bond and *Mission: Impossible* all rolled into one private eye movie and I was chump number one.

They wanted to know what our small business was doing and weren't scared to keep tabs.

I discovered decoys, gambits and more signs than a third base coach would ever have to use during the World Series. They came in, cased the joint and got a feel for operation without letting the cat out of the bag.

Yeah, that's right, I said cat. That's me— the patsy, the pawn — a young editor of a newspaper on the cutting edge of a story. How was I supposed to know what was coming down? It made my fur stand on end.

They came in pairs, straight out of la-la land. One was the

lookout, the other the snitch. While one snitched, the other snatched. They scooped my story before my newsroom knew what hit it. It was on the front page of the rival rag with a byline other than my own, wrapped up nice and neat in a pretty little package. And I couldn't do anything about it.

We were the kingpins, the big daddy, large-and-in-charge and the spooks did what they had to do to take us down. We wanted revenge, but instead of going toe to toe with them, we beat them the newspaper way. That's right, the newspaper way: they take one of our stories, we take two of theirs. They steal a byline, we steal a headline. They send two of our papers to the garbage, we send a drop box full of theirs.

Spy versus spy? Oh yeah, this cool cat has claws. Keep tabs on your competitor's business in an honest way, see, and maybe you can get a feel for what's going down, see? Here are some tips:

Look around. Attend local meetings. Go to town gatherings and mingle with business leaders. Get the drop on what they're up to from the inside. Ask your customers if they shopped around before using your services and you may be surprised to learn what they tell you. Nobody likes a stool pigeon like a competitor. You lookin' at me funny? I didn't think so.

Newsworthy. Read about your industry by subscribing to local newspapers, magazines or relevant business magazines. Check out the ads and you can get the scoop on what your competitors are doing. Put your own ads in and watch the competitors sweat. Send in Knuckles and Bull if they get out of line. They love that sort of thing.

Spy-der Web. With the Internet, finding out what a competitor is doing is a click away. Information is the name of the game on the Internet and it's easy access. Not only can you discover what the locals are doing, you may get some great ideas from national or out-of-state stores.

This message won't self-destruct in 10 seconds, but it can make a big difference in how you do business. And on the flip side, make sure you don't let the cat out of the bag about your business practices. You never know who might be watching.

Meow.

Blue or black ink ... which is better for business?

A good business communication can seal the deal faster than you can say "Show me the money!" But when it comes to putting a signature on the dotted line, should a black or blue ink pen do the job?

The arguments are simple. For a formal document black is the only way to go. It matches the ink, is a conservative choice and everyone is expecting it. Hey, the Founding Fathers did it on the Declaration of Independence and U.S. Constitution, why can't a small business owner, right?

Blue ink, on the other hand, stands out on a black-inked formal document like Shaquille O'Neal in Munchkinland. Professional baseball players like a blue ink autograph on their baseball cards and my wife uses blue ink to write me letters. But are those good enough reasons to use on for a business document?

Oh, the humanity. Regis, can I please use a lifeline?

Here's my take on the situation: If you want to use a blue pen on day-to-day business transactions, do it. If nothing else, your name will stand out at the bottom of the page and that's enough to make the savviest of business owners happy. After all, remembering your name is what it's all about, isn't it?

Keeping in mind it's all about the looks, here are some other tidbits of useful information when it comes to making your business communication look its best:

Simple Simon. Don't venture outside the blue or black ink arena. While the multi-colored pen your son or daughter has on their bedroom desk may look attractive, don't use it. Reds, greens, purples, gold and any other color kids play with doesn't look professional. In fact, it looks like your kid runs the business, not you.

Autograph it. If it's a simple mailing or correspondence make sure you use your own signature. While computers do a fantastic job of scanning a person's signature, it's still less than the original. Nothing says important like a real signature.

Avoid the felt. Felt tip pens are for the birds. I can't stand it when I get a letter signed by someone who used a thick pen. If I take this much time to write about using a blue or black ink pen, and go out of my way to use one, then the person doing business with me should be as considerate. C'mon, felt?

Time and time again the pen has proven mightier than the sword. If we only knew what color of ink to use, the world would truly be a better place.

Free! Business improvements that cost absolutely nothing

When someone thinks of small business improvements trips to the hardware store and backbreaking hours of weekend work usually come to mind. But the truth of the matter is you can put away the nail apron and hammer because improving your business doesn't have to cost money. Some improvements won't even make you sweat.

By taking the time to work on all the aspects of running a small business that don't cost money, you can turn your small business into one that rivals and exceeds the largest corporation. After all, working on attitude doesn't cost anything. If you practice being optimistic and pleasant, even about the worst job in the building, clients will notice.

Or what about customer service? A good personality and

work ethic can be more beneficial to your business than the most expensive computer system. I'm loyal to business owners who go the extra mile to make sure I'm satisfied. That usually means nothing more than follow-up phone calls or just a quick note here or there making sure I'm content.

Keeping your store or office clean doesn't cost more than a little elbow grease. I'm impressed with businesses that take pride in their appearance. There are scores of paying customers who would like to do business with clean establishments.

But don't take my word for it. Try it and see for yourself. What do you have to lose?

Thinking about working from home? Here are some ideas to help you with your decision

Working at home sounds great. As a writer and graphic designer I could be very productive from my home office. I have the computer, printer and a phone line. Everything I need to be a successful telecommuter is right there.

On the other hand, I live minutes away from the office — so close I can go home for nice lunch and watch and an entire rerun of Magnum P.I before I'm late. Most people would dream of my situation, but many more would give it up in a minute to work at home.

At home you could stay with the kids, work in a comfortable surrounding and at your own pace. It's a commuter's dream, but have you ever tried it? It's a lot harder than you think.

I've stayed home with my daughter and tried to get work done. While I finished my project, I went to bed feeling guilty. The idea of strapping yourself to a desk all day while your child fights for your attention is gut wrenching.

So the debate in the Kissman household remains. Should I free up time and work at home or bite the bullet and make the short trip to the daily grind? Here's what I thought about when I made my decision:

Work space. Home-based businesses need a separate workspace. If you don't have one, it may be worth your time to turn the spare area in your garage, bedroom or basement into an office. Working out of your living room gives you too many distractions.

Connections. I have a modem, but it's a simple phone-based hookup. The phone company can only guarantee a 28.8-baud connection. It's frustrating working within those limits when at work I fly with a high-speed connection. If I ever decide to work at home I need my connection updated.

State your business. I can do everything I do at work at home. I'm lucky. Some professions aren't as fortunate so make sure you have everything you need. If you don't have the equipment, it can be a costly way to get started.

Part Two:
Manners and First Impressions

Think running a good, successful business is about crunching numbers and managing an office? Even if you work alone you'll have to deal with people from time to time. Without good grooming, manners or a simple idea of what you're doing, you'll hurt your chance to succeed. So take the gum out of your mouth, sit up straight and pay attention.

First impressions aren't easy to come by. Clean up your act and make it stick

There was a number of reasons I didn't take the man seriously while I inquired about his services. I should have paid attention to every word he said. But I just couldn't bring myself to do it.

It wasn't the way he dressed. He wore an expensive suit with a tie that matched perfectly. He was pleasant enough and spoke quite eloquently. I was quite impressed with him over the phone and in the parking lot where he came out to meet me. He even had some candy he offered me when we got into his office and the pile of paper he called a desk — if he could just find it.

Maybe the candy was under that pile of papers. No, it wasn't there, he said. Maybe it's in this drawer full of wrappers that really shouldn't be here. Nope, not there either. Maybe it's in the file cabinet. Yeah, that's the ticket, he said. If you still want it, I can go get it for you.

I looked at his beautiful oak desk, hand carved with ornate details that Fortune 500 company executives would envy. Too bad, you couldn't see the top of it. My impression of this man went from good to very, very bad.

First impressions are crucial in the business world. Any small business owner worth their salt knows this. Many people realize the importance of being professionally dressed and being well mannered. But impressions go deeper than that, much deeper.

Business owners need to know potential clients are looking

at much more than just one person. They are looking at the entire environment. Keep in mind the things you see everyday are brand new to anyone who walks in the door.

Here are some house cleaning tips:

It's called a trash can, use it. Don't be afraid to throw things away. People hoard outdated documents and other pieces of paper they never use. If it's unused for four months, throw it away.

Stow it, don't show it. If space permits, put all of your supplies out of sight and into cabinets or storage bins. Clients like to check things out while they wait. Don't give them a chance to think about your hygiene.

Clean up. Make sure your work spaces lend themselves to a convenient flow. Keep what you need to operate on a daily basis, i.e. pens, paper, disks and day planner, in order on your desk. If you have to come in early every day or stay late, take a moment or two to clean up. It helps in the long run.

Any place a potential customer can see you is a place where you have the chance to make a good impression. Use that to your advantage and give the customer your best. It just makes good business sense to take a few extra minutes and make sure things are organized.

Who knows? It might just make a deal that much sweeter ...

... just like that piece of candy. (Luckily it was in a wrapper.)

There are many ways to say thank you, pick one and do it

My new suit didn't fit me. Somewhere along the line, from taking it off the rack to taking it home, there was a mistake. It wasn't my fault, and I wasn't pointing fingers, but nobody was taking responsibility. I was getting upset.

The clerk who sold it to me wasn't there. The clerk that was helping me said I was responsible to get it fixed and his manager didn't even offer me an apology when I left. Maybe I expected too much, but my investment needs to pay off. Business suits aren't cheap.

Disgruntled, I left the store with my suit and went directly to a tailor near my house. I told the tailor my story and threw the suit on the counter while pleading for them to work their magic. The tailor smiled and said no problem.

She said she'd work on it right away and we'd have it the next morning. My wife had to hold me up because I almost fainted.

I decided to write a letter to the owner of the tailor shop, letting him know what a fine job his employee did with me. The tailor went out of her way to make sure I was happy, even though it wasn't her fault the suit wasn't right.

Small business owners don't always get the chance to be around the office and good customer service may happen without them knowing. At the same time, when doing business with others, someone may go out of their way to treat us in an exceptional manner.

Imagine how you'd feel as an employer to know one of your customers felt trust toward your company because the actions of an employee. That should be enough to inspire you to go out of your way to make sure the business you are dealing with knows the effect their employee has on you. Besides writing a letter, here are some other ways to make sure employees get noticed:

Call out the manager. In a situation where you were displeased, most people wouldn't hesitate to call the manager and give them an earful. Do the same when someone does something wonderful. Call out the manager and let them have it. Imagine the look on the employee's face when they discover you were praising them the whole time.

Use the phone. Personal phone calls are a good way to say thanks. This way you get the chance to know the owner of the business or start a beneficial friendship. Maybe a successful business relationship can prosper. You never know.

Send a card. Hey, it works on birthdays, why not send one when you get superior service? A nice card does wonders. But don't stop there. Depending on how much you want to put into saying thank you, flowers, candy or even a stuffed toy would be appropriate.

After writing that letter, I quickly got a reply from the owner of the store. He said he would reward his talented employee for handling my problem so professionally. I felt good about that. It also felt good to know that every time I stepped foot in that store, the employee would know that I appreciate her service and she may try even harder to get my stuff done.

Not a bad deal for writing one letter.

Manners are everything when eating a business lunch

The first bite of salad is always the best. Everyone knows that.

It's because you have a full range of options of which part of your salad you want to eat. You could choose the part that doesn't have a lot of salad dressing and go for a dry approach or dive right in and immerse yourself in the part drowning in Ranch.

I chose the latter. I filled my fork with salad and shoved it into my mouth. Sitting through a conference agenda is tough, requiring more attention than I'm willing to give. It doesn't matter what the content, I can only absorb so much of the same thing before I lose interest and think about other things. And for day-long conferences, those other things I think about are the meals. In this case, lunch.

As soon as I took my first bite, a woman sat down in the open seat next to me. She quickly introduced herself, waiting for me to do the same. Up until that moment I was enjoying the best bite of salad ever. From that moment on I felt like a hatchling eating my mother's regurgitation.

It's very awkward when someone asks a question while you're chewing. If you're polite, you cover your mouth, mumble an apology, then move your neck back and forth while trying to swallow the food whole.

I forced a swallow and made my introduction. I was the first to sit at the table, but quickly found myself surrounded by four other people. From then on, I nibbled at my food, ready for any conversation to leap from the table.

Here are some tips for business lunch etiquette:

Don't be the loudmouth. The first thing I notice at a table is the dominant voice. It's usually a man with a booming bass, but I've heard women who dominate just as much. When you have a loudmouth sitting at your table it's hard to hear anyone else, especially when you're involved with individual conversations. If someone across the table asks you a question, then it's OK to unleash your voice. Mediation is key here. Know when enough is enough.

Avoid the drip. When I get the chance to meet people, I want them to remember me for my accomplishments or current status. Not because I have salad dressing dripping from my lips. Order something that doesn't drip or flake easily. Take your time eating and be conscience that something could spill. Don't be afraid to wipe the mouth often. A clean mouth is a happy mouth.

It's OK to eat. It really is. A lot of people decide to hold their conversation as long as they can and never eat their food. Personally, if I'm having a conversation with you, I still know you're listening if you are chewing. If you wait until the conversation is over, the food might be cold or removed because of time constraints.

I left the conference with more information than I could possibly use in a lifetime. Even more importantly, though, I went away with business contacts and friends because I took time to talk with them during lunch. Despite being one of the harder settings to find out about people because of all the commotion, it is a rare opportunity to have somebody's attention for a set amount of time.

Know your cell phone etiquette

Just because a person owns a cell phone doesn't mean they know the polite way to use it. If that were the case my fear of public speaking would be a thing of the past.

Whoever said people are more afraid of public speaking than anything else must have had me in mind. I don't mind the actual speaking if I have a good topic to talk about, but I still get very, very nervous. Thinking about it makes me sweat.

So was the case when I was talking to a group about the importance a publication can play in an organization. I was fighting a case of the jitters, butterflies and knock-knees, all at the same time, when I stepped to the lectern.

I made it through the first part of my well-rehearsed speech without a problem. The audience loved it and I wasn't even mumbling. The second part, however, was another story. Just when I thought I was about to put my speech into cruise control, a cell phone rang in the front row.

It was loud and threw me for a turn. I lost my train of thought and stuttered to regain it. I had to find my place on the page and start over, repeating a point I made earlier.

If this was the only interruption, I may have been able to salvage the final part of my speech, but that was not to be on this fateful day. Instead, the man who answered the phone, who happened to be in the first row, carried on a conversation while I tried to talk.

Ownership of a cell phone has responsibility. Here is what should always be remembered:

It's OK to turn them off. When you're in a meeting, at a speech, on a golf course or in a place where other people may be trying to listen or watch as a group, turn the phone off. It's rude to interrupt. If the phone can't be turned off, stay at the office.

Private talk. If you happen to find yourself in a meeting with the phone on and it rings, leave to answer it. Don't decide to have a meeting within in a meeting.

Car phones. Cell phones are a problem in cars. If you can't maintain a constant speed or direction you shouldn't use the cell phone. Causing a crash because you needed to make sure someone turned off the lights is poor judgement.

I made it through the speech that day despite the interruption. It was definitely a learning experience. Everyone in the room glared at the guy with the cell phone. He eventually got the picture and hung up.

From that I learned that people's second greatest fear — the fear of dying — was enough to make the guy scurry out of the room. I guess he thought the icy stares everyone was shooting him could really kill.

The best tip of all is to know what you're doing

Coming from a town of five thousand people, I never had a reason to ride in a taxicab. Our taxi was the backseat of my mom's minivan while on the way to the grocery store. Never would I think of tipping her.

Yet, as I sat in the backseat of a Chicago cab, I wondered

why I didn't, or at least ask mom what a fair tip was because I didn't have a slightest clue.

I was getting nervous. Not only did the cab driver keep glancing back at me in his rear-view mirror, but I knew we were close to my destination. I kept looking at the meter and tried to calculate exactly how much I should give him.

My mind raced. My palms were sweating.

Fifteen to twenty percent sounded to high. But that was exactly what waiters receive. He isn't a waiter, though.

I'd give a parking attendant a dollar or two, but this guy wasn't fetching a car, he was driving one. That had to be worth a few extra dollars.

Airline porters get a dollar a bag. I knew that one. But after looking out my window and not seeing an airport anywhere, that wasn't going to work. Besides, it was just me and I was on my way to a conference.

If I were with someone I'd ask him or her what they'd do. That's always a good way to make sure you aren't tipping too much, or even worse, tipping too little. It's a fine line between rewarding and insulting someone who is performing a service for you.

It's also important to remember anyone who performs a service can be tipped. This includes hotel maids, who usually get about a dollar or more per night; tour guides might gets as much as five dollars for a long trip, if the tip isn't included, and bellboys get about a dollar a bag.

I couldn't for the life of me remember how much to tip a cab, though. This guy was doing a good job. He kept the speedometer no more than 20 miles over the speed limit, which judging by the other taxis whipping by us, was pretty safe.

He didn't hit another car or any pedestrians. That was a plus, too.

So when he delivered me to my destination safely, I tipped him pretty well. It was about four bucks.

I was worried that wasn't enough at the time and checked

with some colleagues to find out if I gave him too much.

They said that was about right.

I replied, "Hey, that's a good tip."

Sweeten the pot to get in good with your co-workers

The itch always starts on the bottom part of the nose. It's a tingling sensation merely letting you know something is about to happen. It's an opportune time to brush the area and end the misery, but that isn't an option for a new employee on the first day of work.

Being mistaken as someone who picks a nose isn't a good way to start. So the tingle is ignored and the office tour begins. Try to focus on where the boss is taking you, but it becomes more difficult. The tingle switches to a twitch. The rest of your body is begging for your brain to give the go-ahead for a scratch, but the brain refuses. It's uncomfortable and may become unbearable.

But there's so much information to take in your first day of work. New colleagues introduce themselves and you have to remember their names. And the bathroom, can't forget where that is. After all, first impressions are everything. You don't want to get lost on the way to the john.

While your tour ends, sweat trickles down your face. You make it back to your desk and mercifully, your boss leaves. It's time to scratch like you've never scratched before.

It feels so good to relieve the pressure. Your body thanks you and your brain lets you scratch a little longer than normal. Well, actually too long because your boss brought the rest of the staff over for a hearty and final hello.

Welcome to work.

Now that you may have been embarrassed and will surely

remember this day for the rest of your life, it's time for some damage control.

These tips are for just that occasion, and any other awkward work situation:

Sweetness. Put a little candy dish on your desk. Your co-workers will make a point to come over and nibble on your snacks. They'll also chat with you and thank you for your offer. Pick good candy, though. Don't use leftover Halloween candy or stale goodies. Have plenty of it, too. You'll never believe how good this works until you try it.

Lunch it. Taking a couple of co-workers to lunch is a good way to break the ice. No one at my workplace turns down a free meal and I can't believe we're all that different from other working environments.

Don't be shy. Make as much conversation as you can with your new co-workers. Chat during breaks or on the way to the parking lot. Make yourself available for conversations, too.

So there you have it. Time-tested ideas to make your new job much more enjoyable. And by all means, ditch the itch as soon as you can.

Take it from someone who nose.

Excuse me, but are business interruptions really necessary?

No one likes interruptions, but sometimes they're a necessary evil in the small business workplace. Deadlines, waiting clients and phone calls interrupt a meeting for the sake of business. The important thing is to make sure —

You're absolutely right, Tim.

Excuse me?

Don't let me interrupt, I hate it when people do that. Please continue.

As I was saying, there's a time and a place to interrupt. Columns usually aren't the best time or place no matter what it is you have to say. It doesn't matter —

What if what I have to say is really important?

Then you wait until I'm done. I'm trying to write about interruptions. You couldn't have picked a worse time to bug me.

Sorry. I'll wait.

What did you want?

Pardon?

What did you want? You interrupted me, now tell me what you want.

It can wait.

You're sure?

Yes, please continue. This is very interesting. I can't wait to read your three tips. I find those very informative and helpful.

Anyway, there are times and places to interrupt — depending on the importance of the message. Emergencies, of course, override all these rules. Coffee, on the other hand, doesn't.

That was funny.

Are you finished?

Yes.

Here are a few tips:

Closed doors. When the door is closed it's best not to open it. It's closed for a reason and unless an emergency happens, or the office owner tells you it's all right to interrupt in advance, avoid the door like a pink slip.

Don't assume. Don't hover around a doorway or barge into a meeting to get attention. I hate that. If the person you want to see is in a meeting, wait. Don't interrupt what they are doing, it will just make the available time more scarce.

Or make short columns longer.

Those are fighting words, buddy. Keep it up.

Respect. The bottom line is to do unto your co-workers, as you would like them to do to you. It doesn't matter their title, be it intern or CEO; we all have certain rights that should be respected by everyone in the office. No one deserves to be interrupted.

Well said.

Now what was it that you wanted to say?

You know, it was so long ago that I forgot.

Figures.

The 'uh's' have it, but it doesn't mean it's right

The difference between a good businessperson and a great one is a little thing I like to call the "uh." It's the out-loud pause a speaker takes before finishing a thought.

The good ones may use it, the great ones never do.

Granted it's not the worse thing a person can do when speaking. Having lunch left in your teeth, bad breath or a stain on your collar ranks higher than a simple "uh."

When having a potential sale or long-lasting business relationship on the line why take the chance of sounding off? The "uh" is a cancer on speech and very distracting. Do you tune in when a professional athletes puts "uh," or "ah," or some silly catch phrase like, "you know what I mean?" in an interview?

"Uh, that's right. You know what I mean, when it rains, uh, it pours. Like I said, uh, we did it once we did it, uh, again."

I've thrown many a remote control in disgust after watching one of these "uh-tterly" terrible interviews. If I had a remote control at every business function I attended, I'd do the same because just about everyone is guilty of the "uh-fense."

Here are some tips to help you through the tough times on stage or at a business mixer:

Choose 'em. Choose words carefully when speaking. If it's a speech, write them in advance and practice what to say. It reduces the chances of an "uh" and allows you to make eye contact with your audience and not the hotel's stationary.

Watch your speed. Don't talk too fast, or for that matter, too slow. Talk in a natural tone and speed. It projects a comfortable image to listeners, especially if it's a one-on-one conversation.

Be aware. Know how you sound. Practice in front of a mirror. Grab a spouse, child or a pet and run your speech by them or just practice casual conversation. Even if you think you've mastered the speech it doesn't hurt to keep your talents sharp.

Everybody says an "uh" at sometime. It's a natural way for your mouth to catch up with your brain. That doesn't mean it should be a habit.

Common area etiquette: We're not your mothers!

At home it may be all right to leave a candy wrapper on the counter or splash a drop or two of milk on the floor — you'll clean it later, right?

Sure, but leave the thought at home. Think that way in the office and you're in trouble. If you leave a common area disorganized you'll hear the classic response from someone who takes pride in cleanliness: "We're not your mothers!"

Being a slob is annoying, demeaning and unflattering.

In a small business environment everyone has to pitch in and help clean, straighten up or organize the common areas. Employees who continually clean up after co-workers feel slighted and may resent their job.

As an employer you could have a morale problem on your

hands. Not to mention the dirty kitchen and office you'll have when the people who were kind enough to clean stop doing it. Unless it's specifically in their job description don't expect your employees to pick up after you. Do it yourself!

I had to turn to an expert, my mom, to get some tips for this one. Accuracy is next to godliness … or is it cleanliness? Whatever the case, here's what can be done to make sure office common areas are kept clean:

Use disposable. One of the easiest ways to encourage people to clean is to use disposable plates and utensils. It's far easier for people to toss paper plates than to scrape them off and either wash them or put them in a dishwasher.

Plastic is just easier to use and so simple to clean up that even the laziest person may be inclined to do it. Even you, Tim.

Stick with the script, Mom.

Be smart. Know that when you eat, crumbs or scraps are going to be left behind on the table or counter. Water may spill, and if you don't use a coaster, a ring will form. For some reason these simple facts are thrown out the window and forgotten at the office by the smartest of executives.

A warm washcloth and a little patience can clean up the dirtiest kitchen. Just make sure to look at the space you left behind. If it's messy, clean it. This is something Tim never learned.

Mom, if you keep it up you're not coming back.

Organize. Another way to keep areas clean is to put someone in charge of doing it. A chart can designate a new person every week or day to clean an area. I'm not even going to guess what my mom is going to say.

I don't like it. You should be able to clean up your own mess. Remember that time you and your brothers were playing and —

That's all the space we have for this column. Keeping common areas clean just takes a little compassion for your fellow employee. It's a lesson everyone should learn.

Don't make me sic my mother on you.

Tim doesn't really mean that, he's just trying to come up with a clever ending. I'm so proud of him.

Mom, stop it.

A neat looking business is the way to profit

On my way to work, I have the unfortunate luxury of driving past a homeowner who decided long ago to dump appliances, cars, metal and anything else he could think of in his front lawn. The pile of garbage towers above the house and threatens to spill into the road.

Businesses, who share the same street, especially in small downtowns with storefront windows lined up next to each other, share a similar problem when owners let their appearances slip. While some businesses may not need to be as sterile or neat as a hospital, when sharing space with neighbors, keep your storefront neat. Every business depends on the look of a town and the stores within it.

The best communities have clean downtown areas with thriving small businesses. These communities share ordinances for the height and color of signs, mandate updated and clean storefronts and sponsor banners and other citywide initiatives promoting pride.

It's too late for the property owner because he'll never change till he moves because of a grandfather clause. However, it's not too late to make improvements to your storefront and help make your town a better place to live — and best of all, shop.

Here are some tips:

Display and rotate. This one is easy for retail shops. Make sure to change the way your window looks at least once a month. I like seeing scenes or similar themes in a window. If it works for the big department stores in New York, imagine what it can do for small town, Michigan. Just use your imagination and have fun.

Clean it up. When you rotate the display, clean the windows on the inside and outside. People don't like dirt. Shoppers like clean surroundings and if your store looks dirty they won't go in. Sweep the sidewalk and keep the outside of your establishment looking neat, too.

Form a club. I think one of the best things a small business owner can do for their community is to become involved. Have annual contests for the best kept window or most improved storefront. A group of successful business owners can make a big difference to help the community and in the end, help themselves.

Unless you're a junkyard, keep your business property looking neat. After all, customers want to peek inside and see what you're selling, not count the rodents running around.

Leaving voice mail messages revives stuttering memories

Leaving voice mail messages makes me nervous. Just like when I used to stumble and mumble through a phone conversation with a girl for the first time. I always plan on speaking to whom I'm calling, but when they aren't in and the only option is to leave a message, my tongue becomes thick, my thoughts become blurred and I get dizzy.

My high school life flashes before my eyes.

Uh, hello, this is, er, Tim Kissman, and I, um, well, would like to know if - I mean if you're not too busy - maybe you and I could <hiccup> sorry, I get the hiccups when I'm nervous ... maybe we could go to a movie together or something like that.

If the person were on the line, I'd have no problem stating my business and getting on with the day. But when the machine kicks in, I feel the pressure of making sure to leave a quick message, without pausing.

Tim Kissman, I, sit, well I used to sit behind you in history. <hiccup> I'm the one with the feathered hair ... yeah, that's me ... I, uh, was just calling to see if you'd like to see a movie with me ... that is if you're not too busy.

Leaving a message usually throws me into an unwanted and aggravating game of phone tag, but the business world survives on the answering machine and if you can't leave a good message, you won't seal the deal. Much less pass on the important information you need to do your job.

Here are tips for leaving the perfect message:

Plan ahead. Like everything else, going into the message with a plan is a good way to keep mistakes to a minimum. Organize your message by stating who you are, why you are calling and how to reach you, and then fill in details later. I like to repeat my name and number at least twice during the message — not because I'm careless, but because it gives the listener a chance to write it down without replaying the tape.

Clearly the way. Speak clearly, don't mumble and get rid of pauses. Less is always more because no one likes to hear long messages. If you know it's going to be long, just tell the person to call you back to discuss the matter further.

Give it a chance. Once you leave the message, the recipient will probably listen to it, unless they are on vacation or away from the office for other reasons. Don't call back and leave another until you give them sufficient time. I'm scared to do this so it's not a problem for me, but I know I hate getting repeat messages from people who don't give me a chance to respond. It drives me nuts.

I thought we'd see the new Batman, I hear the Penguin is in it. He's my favorite villain ... why are you laughing? It's supposed to be good ... no? ... uh, your great, great *grandmother is in town? <hiccup> <hiccup> Well, uh, you can't duck out of that, maybe some other time. Thanks anyway. <hiccup> ... hello?*

Part Three:
Sound Good, Look Good

Is there a 12 a.m. or 12 p.m.? No, there shouldn't be. Not when you're advertising to the public. If you're open from 8 a.m. to 12 p.m., please use noon. Or if you're open until one minute past 11:59 p.m., tell the world you close at midnight. Using 12 a.m. or 12 p.m. is confusing and makes me want to scream. Thank you and please take a look at these other ideas that could separate your business from the rest.

A newsletter is a way to make bill days OK

My former boss plowed into the room. She didn't have her pleasant demeanor about her. Usually she was in control; calm, cool and collective, ready for anything that a small business owner could handle.

But on this particular day she was coming apart at the seams. It looked like she was ready to commit suicide with an electric razor — totally out of place for someone with such a positive attitude.

Being the observant second-in-command, I asked what was wrong. The question didn't register while she turned her computer on, so I asked again. This time she turned and shot daggers through me with an icy stare. She muttered the words that send shivers through all small business owners: "It's bill day."

Bills needed to go out the door and this meant spending a couple hours in front of a computer, a few more making sure the billings were right and then the time spent stuffing envelopes. A process we hated as much as the customers did receiving them.

Knowing bill day was dreaded, we decided to brainstorm a way to make it more interesting. Through the course of the session, we decided to include a corporate newsletter with our billing.

It made perfect sense. We realized we had a market audience with our billing list and they have to open the mail because it's a bill (at least we hoped). While we have their attention, why not let them know more about us? We made it interesting by telling clients about upcoming specials and including fun facts with short stories about the business.

Our philosophy was simple. Try to make a boring task interesting. And it worked. We saw an increase in sales and people felt they could trust us. When we visited our clients we'd see our little articles clipped and put on bulletin boards. How many times have you seen regular ads clipped out and displayed? Almost never.

Here are some other ideas to incorporate into your newsletter:

Simplicity is divine. Don't overload the recipient with information. Pick a theme for every mailing and stick to it. If you have an early Christmas special coming, use that as a starter. Pick one or two stories about a personal experience or something your business has done. Photos are great if you have the technology, but aren't essential.

Pick a color. Use color to make a statement with each newsletter. It can be as simple as using a colored paper or different colors in the text. The most effective newsletters I've seen are printed on the front and back of a single sheet of colored paper.

Free tips. If all else fails and there's nothing to write about, include a free tip about your business. Make it a big secret you are letting out of the bag. If you work in retail, reveal how you choose what's on sale or how to decorate a window properly. There are hundreds of trade secrets that could be revealed to customers.

Bill days have reached legendary proportions. The newspaper industry is a strange one and it makes for good stories. But that doesn't mean other small businesses aren't interesting, too. It just takes some creativity and a desire to reach out to clients. The newsletter not only informs and entertains; it's a way to let your customers know a little about you.

Proofread your copy carefully

At one time or another small business owners are going to have to right, I mean write, something. It could be something as simple as an inter-office e-mail or as difficult as a letter to the company's most important clients. Either way, it pays to proofread.

Everything that goes out of your office should be red, I mean read, by as many people as possible. There's nothing that turns off educated readers more than poorly written copy.

Be careful about who reads your copy. I've been in offices where proofreaders see it as there, I mean their, mission to find as many mistakes as they can and rub it in your face. Never mind they can't write a grocery list without making an error but when it comes to other people's copy, watch out — they have eagle eyes. Make sure it's someone who nose, I mean knows, something about the English language.

Some writers are turned off when their work is proofread. They feel others don't understand what they're trying to say or, in the very least, take it personally when a correction is made.

I believe people who do their best to find typos are also doing their best to help the writer look his or her best. It's an opportunity to shine when typos are found and eliminated

This doesn't mean it's OK to make mistakes. When you write, no matter what it is, you should do your best to keep it error-free and neat. Typos don't have to be a way of life. Here are some steps to take to avoid them — or at least make them less noticeable.

Spell check. Use you're, I mean your, computer's built-in spelling and grammar check. It's a lifesaver. Everyone slips from time to time on the keyboard. Your first line of defense can save you a lot of editing time later. I no, I mean know, it helps me.

The loop. Use every employee you have to check your

work. I believe the more the merrier. Obviously some items are OK to go out the door with one quick proofread but, if it's important, different eyes can help catch different mistakes.

Outside help. If none of the above applies, get outside help. There are many businesses that specialize in writing that will be glad to take a look at your copy for a free, I mean fee.

So their, I mean there, you have it. Simple advice from a writer who has probably jinxed himself with typo advise, I mean advice.

One last thought: Dictionaries, thesauruses and any other grammar books are also invaluable. Never leave hone, I mean home, without them.

In the business world it pays to choose your words carefully

I had to stare at the invitation sitting on my desk.

It fit perfectly inside a matching envelope, sealed with wax. The expensive paper was etched with gold borders and handwritten in flowing calligraphy, no doubt meant to catch the attention of the recipient. Somebody took a great deal of time to put these invitations together. I was impressed.

However, I remembered right then to never judge a book by its cover. How true that piece of advice was for this invitation. While dazzled by the appearance, I was frightened by the content.

It took too many words to let me know I was invited to a local politician's open house. I don't know if he was attempting to sound elegant, but I couldn't make heads or tails of the invitation's exact meaning. Good writing is hard to find and it obviously wasn't contained in this invitation.

"Enclosed herewith is an invitation to an event for which you are cordially invited. Pursuant to this please find an enclosed reply card to send back in order to properly reserve a spot at our table."

Huh?

I'm glad I was an English major in college because at first I didn't quite understand what this meant. The idea that we live in the 21st century and not the 18th century had something to do with it, too. That person had to use 36 words to say "Come to my event, but please respond so I can hold a table."

Here are some effective ways to write better business communications:

Write in plain English. This is the simplest rule to follow; yet it's always the first one forgotten. I've yet to hear anyone use herewith or pursuant in a casual conversation, so why use it in business writing? Write what you say. Imagine talking to someone when you write. It comes out clearer and more concise, two things that make writing interesting and better.

Use an active voice. It takes fewer words to write in the active voice. The sentence order for the active voice is subject-verb-object. Try that order and you'll find it becomes easier with practice.

Keep it short. If you're writing a best-selling novel or a scathing manifesto, long sentences are all right. But for business writing, sentences need to be simple and concise. They should pack a punch and keep the reader's attention. When writing more than a page, try to break up large paragraphs into smaller ones.

These are just some simple rules. There are as many writing rules in the English language as there are words. You don't have to memorize all of them, but to know as many as possible can add to your skills. If your skills improve, co-workers, subordinates, employers and clients won't shy away from your business.

In fact, they may even come uninvited.

Tim Kissman

Colors keep your small business publication fresh

Creative people dream in vivid color.

I'm interested to see what category I fit in as the writer, graphic designer and editor of my association's newsletter because when I sleep at night my dreams bask in the glow of a PANTONE 201 sun.

My retinas are burned in the maroon-shaded color. Oranges, tennis balls and highlighters look maroon. Maroon bananas don't taste the same and neither does maroon milk.

I face this color every day and it's a challenge to make SBAM's publications look fresh and inviting within the two-color parameters of our budget. I know small business owners face the same formidable task when they publish a company newsletter, too, but don't despair because it's easy to turn your business' two-color blues into a rainbow of opportunities.

Here's how:

Use it or lose it. Through the course of a newsletter, editors tend to use the same amount of color in the same places for every publication. While it may look nice, you aren't getting the most for your money. Your business is paying for a second color so don't be scared to use it all over the place. Accent as many items as possible with a second color. Also, make graphics or use clip art to bring that color to the forefront. Your readers will thank you.

White space. White is a color, too. The problem is many graphic designers or small business owners who have a hand in their publications, don't realize the impact white space can have on their publications. White space pulls the reader's attention to a piece of information and makes long documents easier to read.

Gradients. Just because you have the privilege to use a color doesn't mean you have to use it at 100-percent all the time. Most page layout programs offer a gradient tool to help use the same color at different shades.

Newsletters are an effective marketing tool. Using one can help increase your sales and let customers know a little about your company at the same time. Make sure to put time into a good design and use of colors that will keep your readers interested.

Be careful, though. With great improvements to your publications it may make other small business owners green with envy.

Or in my case, they'll be PANTONE 201.

Shake things up when you're meeting prospective clients

In the business world, there's nothing more important than a handshake. It can mean the difference between making or breaking the deal.

Too many times business owners fail to realize the impact a handshake can have. A flimsy handshake could be interpreted as a weak-minded individual, while a handshake that breaks bones could be too aggressive and drive business away.

The next time you're at an office gathering with business associates try to keep track of who has the best business handshake. Those who are successful and secure in their profession won't be afraid to show it.

My personal shake falls under the category of confidence, but not too much. I try to grip the shaker's hand firmly and pump the hand, no more than twice, from the elbow. I make sure to look the person in the eyes, too. Sometimes the grip isn't tight or the shaker catches me off guard and before you know it I'm struggling to keep my fingers from being crushed. It's embarrassing.

It seems like a lot of worry over something so simple, but there's a lot riding on it. Here are some other ideas to keep in mind when it's time to grip, grin and shake:

First impressions. At social functions keep your drink and food in your left hand as much as possible. This keeps your right hand warm, dry and free so when the boss or a potential client comes along they won't receive a cold or clammy shake.

One hand works. In the business world use one hand to shake, especially on introductions. I get nervous when people shake my hand with their right hand and clasp it with their left. That's too personal. After I get to know them that may be acceptable, but there's no sense in risking it early in the relationship.

Two and out. Two pumps, please. Any more and you might be sending a mixed signal. This, of course, applies to introductory shakes. If posing for a picture or signing a peace accord it's acceptable to pump more than twice.

In our culture the handshake is important.

Make it count every time.

How to make it in the media

Ever wonder why some businesses appear in the local newspaper more than others? Upset business owners called me all the time because they didn't make it into my newspaper as much as their competitors.

They believed newspapers played favorites with competitors by giving them an unfair advertising advantage. No matter how many times I told them that wasn't true they seldom left with a good impression and remained angry. I explained to them some businesses know they can get the attention they crave by creating a good media relationship with a local newspaper or television and radio station simply by being available.

Over time every small business owner becomes an expert in his or her field. It takes a little effort to increase your credibility, and potentially your sales, by getting others, especially the media, to recognize you as a quotable expert.

All a business owner has to do is write effective press releases and be available for comment. Pay attention to current events, too. If you can handle those essentials, here are some surefire tips to get cozy with your local media:

In the news. Scan magazines or the morning paper to see what trends are developing in your trade. Tailor a press release to comment on those trends. Let the reporter know how those trends can affect the local economy. The more work you do on your end the better chance you have of becoming a media contact.

Know the media. It's a good idea to adapt your message to your targeted media. Know what your local newspaper likes in a press release. The same goes for your local television or radio station. Each outlet can differ from another. Take the time to scout what they need and make sure those requirements are met.

Be available. After you send in the release follow it up with a phone call. Let the reporter know you're available for comment about the release and any other community-related issue that centers on your business. When the reporter calls back have your facts ready.

The smoother you make the transition from being just a storefront on Main Street to the leading expert in your community, the more you will benefit. Having a good media relationship can really help your business. Just think of all the coverage you could get.

And just think of all the phone calls the editor will get from your jealous competitors.

Picture this: A photo is worth more than a thousand words

For every great tip out there to help a small business owner take a professional photo, there are a dozen ways to ruin one. There's no better way to cut off a person's head, have a lamp post grow out of a shoulder or be out of focus than trying to do take a professional picture yourself.

As an amateur photographer I covered the lens with my thumb, took pictures while no one was looking and even made a former mayor look like he was getting shot by a cannon in front of a local Veterans of Foreign Wars home.

I can't count how many times my subjects were out of focus. These are the same pictures I'm supposed to publish in our newsletter or post on our Web site.

Thank goodness for Adobe Photoshop. But then, software can only do so much.

Yet, I kept trying. The major newspapers, magazines and books always have vivid details and moving scenes gracing their pages. Why can't I?

You can read all the manuals you want, but I've come to two undeniable truths. You need practice and the right film. Both the quantity and quality are important. Take as many pictures as you can. Use at least a 400-speed film, and if you're lucky maybe one or two of them will turn out great.

If you clear that hurdle and everything else is crystal clear, just make sure to remove the lens cap. Here are some tips to help get your picture published in your local paper or Web site:

Subject it. The biggest challenge small business owners face is making their pictures interesting. Newspapers don't like the traditional handshake, "grip and grin," pictures. They're as common as a penny and worth about as much in a story. Stage the photo if you have to, but have your subjects do something.

Identify it. No matter what picture you send to the paper it's important to identify the subjects. Print names and places on the back of the photo in a pen that doesn't bleed. Double check the spelling before sending it off, too. If you're wrong, it will be wrong and papers aren't quick to correct your mistake. They will, however, correct their own.

Scan it. The latest way to send pictures is via electronics. Make sure you know the platform, PC or MAC, the newspaper or media wants it in. It's also important to check the format, usually TIFF or JPEG and resolution, usually a minimum of 150 dpi. If you don't know what this means, call your newspaper and they should be more than willing to help.

Photo opportunities come once in a blue flash

My first taste of fame came in seventh grade. I was at a winter camp, taking my turn at rappelling down an old water tower with a photographer from the local paper waiting for me to jump.

I was brave earlier in the day. On the ground, waiting in line for my turn, the tower didn't seem that tall. But when I was ready to jump, dangling over the edge with nothing to hold on to but a nylon rope that felt like a straw in my hands, it was much different. The thought of chickening out crossed my mind.

I cleared my head and leaned backward. My friends were quiet, holding their breath in anticipation. Just as I was to make the leap of faith I heard the familiar click and whir of a camera. I turned my head in the direction of the noise and saw the photographer taking my picture of what I was sure was my untimely death. Great, I thought, more pressure.

I tried to clear my head again, but after a series of clicks and whirs, I said a little prayer and pushed off. I eventually made it down, thanks to quick coaching from the camp's staff and actually enjoyed myself in the process. I may have expressed an interest to go again, but that can neither be confirmed nor denied.

Everything was fine until the next day when the paper came out. On the front page, there was a picture of me dangling over the edge of the tower, all wrapped up in that nylon rope that brought me safely to the ground.

I faced the wrong direction and there's no way my backside was that big. It had to be my snow pants, I said. But my friends didn't believe me. They called me "Chunk" rest of the week. Some of them still do. But as much as I disliked the picture, I did get a lot of compliments. People were clipping out the picture for me, sending me notes that they saw it and even telling me how great I looked.

If I can get that kind of response for a bad picture, imagine what a small business owner can get with a picture that was well planned. Be ready for that photographer's flash or his call.

Here's how:

Stack the stock. Always keep a stack of stock photos in your desk drawer. The best photos used to be simple black and white ones, but with the Internet and affordable technology that's changed. It's a good idea to get color ones made because if you ever have the chance to have it published in a color publication or on the Internet, black and white doesn't cut it. Have a good supply, too. You never know when you might need one.

Picture ops. If you have the chance to stage something for the press, do it. The more control you have, the better. You should also plan on having your own photographer at the event in case the paper doesn't show up. At the very least bring a camera.

Get seen. Attend events with photographers. If it's a big deal in your community, chances are someone will take a picture. Being in the background counts for something. If people you know are going to look at the picture, chances are they are going to recognize you. You may even get a picture credit in the cutline.

Be ready for any chance to get your picture published. Even if it means you have to leap from tall buildings in a single bound. Just make sure you get the picture taken from the front.

That much I know for sure.

Part Four:
Understanding Technology
(or how to keep from pulling your hair out in computer frustration)

Technology has definitely made our lives easier. Why just the other day I sent an e-mail to a colleague stating this fact. He didn't get back to me right away, like e-mailers usually do, so I tried a fax. Still no response. I called and got his voice-mail, so I became concerned and actually drove over to see him. His building lost power and he was helpless, reading a newspaper in the dark of his office. Yeah, technology is great.

Thunder! Lightning! Take care of your electronics

A lightning storm in my house means a long night for me. At the first clap of thunder I race around in the dark, tripping over baby toys, piles of clothes and my cat in a frantic race to unplug the major appliances.

My list is short and quick: First the television, then the stereo. The computer is always last. It's hard to unplug all those cords. But it doesn't stop me from fitting under my desk and yanking the cords from the wall. A well-placed lightning bolt can knock out anything it touches, especially my expensive Macintosh.

The idea of unplugging expensive electronics isn't new. In fact, buried in most user manuals are explicit instructions on how to unplug and diffuse a stormy situation. I follow those instructions to the letter.

But how many small business owners do the same?

I've been at work during some of the worst storms I can remember and my employer insisted on working through the day. Our computer monitors would jiggle and shake when a lightning bolt struck nearby, and I swore I saw smoke in the disk drive, but we couldn't stop.

In retrospect we should have unplugged every computer and waited for the storm to end. It's easier to burn a few hours of the day and keep the biggest investment in your office safe than to have a lightning bolt put you out of commission.

Here are some plans to further prevent a disaster:

Watch your back. Back up as much data as you can on a timely basis. It's far easier to go back to old records and input a day's worth of work than to start from scratch. Computers crash by themselves all the time. Imagine what would happen if it had help from Mother Nature.

Come unplugged. If you know a storm is coming unplug your machines. It's not enough to turn them off or use a surge protector. The best surge protectors in the world can't stop a direct lightning hit. Insurance can replace the hardware, but your data will be deep fried and unusable.

Warrant this. Computer stores usually offer a warranty when you buy their products. It's a good idea to look into it. It can be added insurance in case of a disaster and give you a piece of mind.

So unless your business and computer hardware can withstand the forces of nature, unplug your computers and anything else that can be plugged into a socket and be ready. If Murphy's Law is correct, anything that can go wrong will.

Don't let the Web get you tangled: Sites are easy to do

There's a common misconception floating around the small business that designing a Web site for your business is hard; maintaining it even harder and promoting it next to impossible.

I've heard people say they feel like a fly trapped in the Web. I like the analogy, but it's hardly the case. It's the fear of the unknown that scares small business owners away.

Listen to me people, it's not that hard to build, manage and promote a Web site. It's easier than ever. Before the Internet came into the powerful medium it is today, Webmasters actually had to program Web pages by using a Hypertext Markup Language or HTML.

HTML is a text-only language that actually tells the computer how to designate the text on the page. When individual computer users log onto your Web site, the computer formats the text and how it appears on the screen. That is a bit confusing, however it shouldn't be intimidating. While the Web grew, so has Web-publishing software. Today's programs allow a Web master to lay the page out how he or she wants it, without having to know the HTML language. The program tags it into HTML automatically.

All the Web designer has to do is have creativity and some time to perfect the site. However, just because you know how to make a Web site, it doesn't mean you know everything. There are other factors to consider:

Think objectively. It's important to figure out what you want your site to do before you launch it. It's best to be as specific as possible. Do you want it to sell products? Maybe it's going to provide a service? Whatever the case make sure you have a plan.

Image is everything. The next step is to think of your site's general makeup. In thinking about this, you need to determine who your market audience is. Once you define this, you can decide if you want to make your site flashy, filled-with graphics or just simple text.

Tick, tock. The last, and perhaps most important, aspect of launching a site is figuring out how to promote it and how you will determine its success. List the site with search engines and promote it by word of mouth. As far as measuring its success, you'll have to come up with that. Usually it's based on numbers of pages viewed, Web sales or an increase in the number of customers.

Tell everyone you know about the site and your hits will increase. With the Internet's growth more than doubling itself every month you have the potential to reach a lot of people, which could mean increased profits.

That's one language that's easy to understand.

Saving files often could erase a lot of headache later

It was a bright, sunny day in July when I finished laying out my 120-page manual. Every morning for three months I came in early and stayed late, painstakingly creating the document.

I could recite every word from every page from memory. I knew the page number for every subject. The manual was no longer a job, it had come an obsession. I didn't create a simple user-friendly piece of literature, I created art and at 2:43 p.m. July 19, 1997 it was finished.

I leaned back, clasped my hands behind my head and looked outside through the window. It was beautiful day. Not a cloud in the sky. There was even a bird chirping on a branch near my office.

It was the perfect time to print. I pointed, then clicked, but instead of a spooling icon for my printer, the computer failed and I lost everything. I had to stare at the computer for a moment, letting the gravity of the moment sink in.

More importantly I forgot to save it.

I pounded the keyboard hoping to jar the document loose. I rattled the monitor, hoping it would fall out, but nothing happened. I stuck my head outside and screamed. Then the sky clouded up. The sun was gone. The bird fell off the branch. It was very, very still.

Tim's document was no more.

I learned a lesson that day. No matter what you're working on, if it's on a computer save often.

Here is some advice for back-ups:

Tape works. Try to get a tape-drive backup system. They don't cost much when compared to the other pieces of computer equipment, but they are well worth whatever you pay. Back up all your files on a regular basis.

Red tape, too. Once you establish a pattern for backing up your computers' drives, make sure to use different tapes or disks. Don't use the same disk on Thursday you used Wednesday. It's not a good habit.

Spread the wealth. When saving documents on your hard drive, save them in different places. Have different external files for each saved version of your large document. It makes it easier to find when and if the computer crashes.

I learned my lesson the hard way that day. For the next three days I put in nearly 40 hours, creating the document from scratch. I pretty much hated life. So, please, listen to me. Don't tempt the fates, save without prejudice.

After all, a document saved is a weekend earned.

Getting ready to surf? Make sure you know where it's safe

Getting information on the Internet is easy. Making sure the information is reliable, however, is another matter.

Just because a Web site has free information doesn't mean that site knows what it is credible. With so many Web sites on the Internet vying for your attention, it's becoming more common to see companies claim expertise. Some sites use faulty information and parade it as being accurate.

Take for instance my first Internet-based mistake. With my company's CEO and a vice president in the front seat of a car, I had a printout from an Internet map service to find a location none of us knew. After going through three construction detours and two dirt roads we found out the hard way we were in the wrong place. I went from being a hero in finding the meeting via an unusual route to being very quiet in the back seat as we scrambled to get to our meeting on time.

Here are some ideas to make sure you're getting reliable advice:

Double check. Sometimes it pays to pick up the phone and call the company, find out how they get their information. If the site doesn't display a phone number or contact person that could be a sign they aren't reliable.

Rev up the engine. Use several search engines to find a site. It's a way to cross-reference the information. At the very least, the site took the time to get registered. Still, verify the facts before taking them to heart.

Practice purpose. Sites that exist to advertise a product may not be entirely accurate. They may appear to have accurate information, but in reality they just pitch their product. In other words, the information is slanted. These sites don't exactly provide the best information. Just be wary.

Buying new office technology shouldn't take rocket science

If my father-in-law, Roger, is any indication, home-based or one-person business owners are very set in their ways. This is especially true when it comes to purchasing technology for their business.

I think it would be easier to build a spaceship and fly to Mars then talk Roger into buying a new computer for his insurance agency. Roger's computer, a 386 PC, isn't keeping up with his software demands. He can run vital programs but they take a long time to process and he doesn't have any Internet capability because of ultra-slow modem speeds.

New business software puts a high demand on memory, more so than computers made three or four years ago. The older computers can run new software, but it would be more interesting, and much quicker, building a spaceship with toothpicks.

Roger knows this, but it's the cost he can't justify.

Here's where the debate, and the plans for my trip to Mars, begins.

I tell him he'll save time not having to wait for programs to run. New programs and a new computer would streamline many of his day-to-day office activities.

He says that would help a little, but it still needs to do more.

I wrinkle my forehead, diving deeper into my sales pitch. I tell him he'll have a faster modem with a new computer. With that you can build a Web page, save money on faxes and have the potential of becoming a bigger agency.

He says that's a good idea, but it still needs to do more.

I scratch my chin. Mars is much too easy a trip. Saturn would probably be a comparable challenge. I mention the viruses that target computers as a last, desperate measure.

He agrees on that one. That does worry him.

When it comes to buying new technology, most home-based or one-person business owners have more questions than they do answers. Here's what to ask before making the purchase:

Will it reduce expenses? This question depends on your business. Studies show paper usage increases with a computer in the office. The initial cost may be hard to swallow, but the time saved and efficiency in the future may outweigh that concern.

Will it increase my income? It could increase it a lot. Doing your printing from powerful word processing programs, paying checks in-house and faxing from a high-speed computer modem will reduce costs. Add that to programs specifically tailored to your business and your bottom line could be much better.

What about saving time? Most times the answer will be yes, but make sure you know how to use what you are getting or else the early stages of your new technology may cause a lot of lost time in learning the system. The smoother the transition the better. Once you learn the software, the real magic begins.

Is it easier to fly to Mars? That's the question that seems to creep in my head when Roger and I talk about his computer situation. I don't think it is. He's trying to run his business the way he knows how and if anyone knows what his business needs, he does. When he's ready to purchase a new computer, he'll do it.

Which is good, because Mars isn't easy to get to …

… even if you have a good computer leading the way.

When Web technology talks make sure you listen

At a recent small business conference I was involved in a conversation I couldn't believe was taking place. Small business owners were huddled around a computer listening to a Webmaster of a very successful small business explain how to make money over the Internet.

His speech was enthralling. He was giving away secrets like candy at Halloween. What took many online marketers years to master, he was gift wrapping and handing out to his crowd of onlookers. I was glad to hear him because he did make a lot of sense.

Unfortunately, I was the only one.

Too bad, too.

Once our knowledgeable speaker finished his presentation, he opened the floor for questions. I thought it would be a great time for the other business owners to find out what they could do to tap the vast resources of the Internet. Instead, they peppered him with skepticism about the Internet 'fad.'

They said it takes too much time to create and run a Web site. They complained promoting a site is never cost justified. For a small business to take time out of an already jam-packed day to advertise a Web site just wasn't worth it to some of my colleagues.

The speaker told the crowd they were overreacting and they could make money by doing three simple things to attract more hits, more business and make more money.

Make it write. Write articles about your business and post them online. If you're a successful small business owner, you know something about what you are doing. Use that knowledge and share it about your business. Believe it or not people get online to look for information like that.

Promote, promote, promote. Like real estate, location is everything when promoting your Web site. You don't need a full time staff to do it, either. If you have a Web site, put the address on your letterhead, business cards and anything else you can think of. Tell people about it when they call and give clients a discount if they go through the Web page to purchase your product. That will generate traffic and boost sales.

Customer list. Send e-mail notices about your products or services to people who show an interest in your company. Make it a weekly note or whenever you there is a sale. If you want, you could even create a small e-mail newsletter for your clients. Tell them about your new endeavors and little facts about what you are up to. The more you reveal, the more they know and trust your business.

Eventually the speaker managed to get some of the small business owners on his side. Thankfully, some took notes about what the Webmaster was saying.

The Internet is the future and virtually untapped by small businesses. It takes some know-how and little time, but that could be the difference between a good and mediocre year.

Using the overhead in an effective manner can make anyone feel super

The overhead projector is like kryptonite. The very stuff that makes Superman, super-less. If you've ever been part of a business presentation with an overhead you know exactly what I'm talking about.

When the speaker uses the overhead correctly, it empowers the audience. I know when I see someone using it effectively I take better notes, process more information and pay attention. I remember everything the speaker talked about and leave with a feeling of accomplishment. I felt like I could leap tall buildings with a single bound, run faster than a locomotive and — wait a second, look up in the sky … is it a bird? … a plane? … no, it's … Super Tim!

I've also seen the ugly half of the overhead. The presentation sapped my attention, bled the effectiveness of the speech and made my head hurt. I felt like Superman on kryptonite — dangerously tired and drained.

I remember reaching out for help to the people sitting next to me. I wanted someone to pull the plug on the diabolical machine before it completely robbed me of my mental strength. But the person to the left of me was already asleep, drooling down the side of his face and snoring. It was the last thing I remembered before losing consciousness.

Lex Luthor would have been proud of that speaker.

There are a lot of ways to avoid the Lex Luthor syndrome even before setting up the machine. Probably the most important is to know how many people are scheduled to attend. If there are more than fifty people, you might need a different way to present your facts. Handouts are a nice way to reach that kind of crowd.

The overhead, though, is nice for meetings with less than fifty people. People don't have to use their x-ray vision to see the overhead, which would be set up across the room from some.

Here are some tips to make sure the audience is seeing green:

Go with the flow. Flowcharts and narrative are a very effective tool. It's good to have a visual that compliments the spoken word. It can clarify what the speaker is talking about and allow the audience a chance to make a mental image, too.

Keep the intensity. If you really want to keep your audience in the loop use different colors. Start with cool colors like blue and green and build up to the warmer colors of yellow, orange and red. Likewise, if you want to de-emphasize something, use black or gray.

Two heads are better than one. Two projectors are twice as effective. Use one projector for the overall outline, and the other for supporting details. Two projectors allow the audience to keep pace with the speaker.

No other presentation device has the potential to make or break a seminar like a projector. Use it effectively and in the interest of your audience. Otherwise, you'll go from super hero to villain in the same amount of time it takes to flip your projector's switch on.

Why wasn't my computer infected?

Computer viruses affect the nation on a regular basis, crippling the giant companies and ruining the smaller ones. I feel for those affected, but still have one nagging question lingering in the back of my hard drive.

Why wasn't my computer infected?

Viruses attack a computer's e-mail system and spread by replicating themselves through the infected computer's e-mail list, sending it out to unwilling victims. Like me. Or at least I thought. I never got a message, though.

I have to imagine someone, in the millions of infected computers out there, had to have my e-mail address. If not that someone, maybe the someone who was on their e-mail list. Or maybe that someone's someone.

Am I really that unpopular? Or am I just lucky? I'll take either case but I still would have liked to be included. I was the last kid on my block to get the chicken pox and I'll probably be the last computer user to get this virus, too. Oh, well.

Viruses are becoming more popular and despite their familiar methods, they're becoming increasingly powerful. Each time they explode into the limelight and dominate headlines, wiping out companies in their path. It's hard to put blame on any one person besides the hacker who wrote the little devil.

Here's what you can do to make sure you keep your business' computer system safe:

The antidote. Buy one of the dozens of virus protection software packages on the market. Some are better than others so do some research before purchasing one. Regardless, having something is generally better than having nothing at all so it's definitely something to look into if you accept e-mails from the outside world.

Be smart. Make sure not to open anything that looks suspicious, especially if it has an attachment. Many companies have policies about opening attachments and others simply forbid it. That's not a bad idea. Usually brains can make a difference, too. Be smart. In the case of the ILOVEYOU bug, why would your uncle's boss put that in the message line, much less send you an e-mail?

Be vigilant. News agencies and computer security experts love to report they found the latest virus. They tell what the virus is and how to stop it. Pay attention to what they're saying and spread the word to your employees. Let them know what's coming and you can save a lot of time dealing with problems in the future.

If none of these sound good to you, there's always the idea of making sure you're part of my e-mail list. If history is any indicator, it's the safest place you'll ever store your e-mail address.

Printer fairy tales: Someday my prints may come

Do you have the printer blues?

Or maybe the reds, greens, yellows and blacks?

Don't know? Ever send an item from your desktop computer to your printer, sitting no more than three feet away, and wait and wait before it printed?

It doesn't matter if you were in a hurry or had all the time in the world, printers have a mind of their own and print when they want to. I still haven't figured out what goes on inside those connecting cables. Whatever it is, it can slow the busiest small business owner.

The sound of the fan or cartridge kicking in is music to my ears. I've seen co-workers dance and breathe a sigh of relief when they heard the sound. This, of course, came after they stood next to the printer, watching the light blink on and off while it spooled their document. They'd grasp the machine like a podium and drum their fingers to some song playing in their head.

None of it helped, though. They would always be in agony and the only time the printer kicked in would be when they walked away.

I find myself lured to the printer myself after I send a job.

The sounds it makes seduces me after working long and hard on a project. I don't dance or drum fingers, though, I simply stare. Co-workers walk by and tell me a watched pot never boils. I usually answer them in a mocking tone, especially if I was waiting long. My prints will come, I tell them. I just know it.

Here are some printer tips to think about when you're waiting (they may even speed up the process):

Take the time. Always allow enough time to print. Depending on the software program and the project, as well as the printer, large files take a long time to spool and print. You may not have all the fonts loaded on the computer, either. So plan ahead and be ready for a delay.

Shake it. If using a laser printer, don't throw away a near-empty cartridge too quickly. When it starts to show lines on your finished work, take it out, shake it and put it back in. You'd be surprised at how long you can make the cartridges last after they show signs of running out of ink.

Keep it new. For an inkjet printer, don't refill the empty cartridges yourself. If you do it incorrectly you can ruin your printer. It's best to simply buy a new cartridge. But if you are daring there are plenty of sites on the Internet where you can buy replacement ink for less than half the retail price.

Printers have a mind of their own and an attitude to boot. Keep that in mind and you should be fine.

Just make sure no one is looking if you're going to dance.

Part Five:
Human Resources and How to Stretch the Dollar

This section is one of the more creative ones in the book. That's because these ideas aren't exactly a perfect fit when applied to every small business in the world. So take a look and try to see how you can transform these ideas into your business. But keep your voice down. The receipt Nazis are out there waiting to pounce.

Avoiding the receipt Nazis takes some planning and organization

The receipt Nazis are out there. They look like the rest of us, but these fanatical storm troopers, who worship cash register tape like it was a god, aren't like us at all. They live to collect and record receipts.

Everyone who has ever held a job or had to answer to a budget knows the receipt Nazi way. These people could be your boss, a co-worker, a spouse and maybe even a child. They're the number crunchers of the group who love their job. Maybe they love it a little too much, but you can never say anything. Excessive requests are their weapons and scrap pieces of paper are their trophies.

They claim it's for a good reason. Insisting receipts be recorded and stored is their way of making sure a small business or household runs on its tight-budgeted course. The receipt Nazis uphold the oath that too many receipts is better than no receipt at all.

The persistence of these paper warriors is admirable, if not down right annoying. But if it weren't for them, small businesses would turn belly up. Household budgets would be out of whack and chaotic spending would run amuck.

More than the average bookkeeper, the receipt Nazi lives for tax day. It's the day they shine and strut. All the hunting, foraging and pleading for the simplest of records is well worth their effort when they clear the IRS hurdle.

It's hard for the average worker to keep track of these tiny slips of paper, much less keep them in some sort of order. Luckily, the minute you forget the receipt Nazi pounces, reminding you to find that transaction record.

Civilians take heart. There are ways to avoid their wrath. Remembering a few receipt tips can make the difference between constant pressure or a heartfelt thanks.

Tips for the tape:

Organize. If you're like me, wadding up receipts and stuffing them into your wallet or pant's pocket doesn't cut it. Keep them in a secure, organized place. A three-ring binder and plastic sheet protectors work great. This gives you a chance to organize them as expenses and save you time later. You could also use separate loose, plastic sheets as temporary storage in your car, briefcase or purse.

Software. Use your computer to keep track of your expenses and income. Software packages like Quicken are everywhere. Pick one that suits your business' needs and use it. You'd be amazed at how much time you'll save and how easy it is to see how your business or home is doing with the software's charts and graphs.

Ask questions. If you have a question or don't know how to classify a receipt, call your accountant. They'll be more than happy to help.

Here's to the receipt Nazi's of every home and business. Their blitzkrieg tactics make them hated at times, but their results make them one of the most valuable employees a business could have.

Following procedures by the book is important

My relationship with Jennifer Aniston never really had a chance.

We were miles apart, I was a younger man and she didn't even know who I was. But I loved her. Unfortunately, that love couldn't leap the chasm our employee handbook created and I was heartbroken.

Writing an employee handbook is an important part of a small business owner's repertoire. Handbooks are a guideline of employee conduct, providing rules of how work should be done.

Too many small businesses exist without them. No matter how smooth the business may run, it will eventually need a handbook. I know firsthand. I lost my Jennifer because of it.

Years ago, when I started out in the newspaper business, I found myself in the middle of a handbook war. During a staff meeting I made mention to the rest of the staff I had a crush on *Friends* star Jennifer Aniston. I made the remark in passing, but soon found myself getting picture after picture of Jennifer on my desk.

The other staff members cut her picture out of magazines and brought them to me. I put the pictures on the wall around my work area, and sighed. I was in love. For a while everything was fine, nobody complained. I had my little Jennifer shrine operating and my work never suffered.

But then Jennifer and I had some troubles. Another staff person in the newsroom decided she wanted to start a collection of her own, but it was with pamphlets and flyers about civil rights groups. She didn't put just one up either - she plastered them everywhere.

The rest of the newsroom staff complained. Her defense: If Tim can have Jennifer Aniston up, why can't I display these? She had a point and we had to consult the handbook to make sure we both were in our rights to have art on the wall. It turned out we both had to take the pictures down. The staffer was upset, I was heartbroken, but rules were rules.

Here are some other areas to explore:

Include it all. Day-to-day operations of your business should be included in a handbook. Items like general working hours, dress codes, vacations, paid holidays, sick leave, office decorations and maternity options should have a place. It's better to have too many items than to forget something.

Termination. It's an ugly word to employers. If you're worried about the correct language to use, consult an attorney and have them help. A handbook is a mighty weapon against legal action.

Fancy, schmanzy. While it may be a pipe dream for some small business owners to have a deluxe employee handbook that's bound and stitched, it doesn't have to be fancy at all. Depending on how thorough or descriptive you get, it may just be a page or two, typewritten and stapled together.

While I've recovered from my breakup with a television star, and understand why it happened, others may not be so easily convinced. If an ounce of prevention is worth a pound of cure, then every page in an employee handbook equals hours of peaceful office work.

Making the perfect employee

Scientists claim they can rebuild genes, clone animals and possibly erase disease. It's a bold statement, but if it's true, oh boy. It's time for me to look ahead and make a bold prediction about the future. We may be on the verge of finding the perfect employee.

We need to use gene therapy. Use those stem cells, clone those cows and make me a Frankenstein that's going to be worker of the month. No, that's not enough. Try worker of the year. No. Think bigger. Maybe the best worker ever!

There's a gene for everything else, why wouldn't there be one for a great work ethic and brains to boot? If you can get rid of disease, you should be able to get rid of laziness. Let's find the gene that cures employee theft, too-many-breaks syndrome and the popular, sleeping-on-the-job disease.

Too many personal phone calls? Take out the old gene and put a new one in. Lunch breaks could be a thing of the past; remove the gene that makes people hungry. Outlandish? Never. It just may take some time.

Rid one defect another may take its place. Get rid of tardiness and smoking might become a bad habit. If an employee leaves early, you may be able to slice out the bad gene and replace it with one that may contain a multitude of bathroom breaks. By the time you reach perfection employee cloning will be commonplace. You can have the perfect staff. Wow.

So, small business owners hang on, the future is getting close. Until then do your best to employ the people who fit into your grand scheme of things.

An intern could be a valuable asset for any small business

The office rumor mill was famous for turning out some whoppers. Everything from mass firings to raises across the board whispered across the cubicles, spreading like a fire. Most rumors were false, but every now and then true one would surface.

That was the case when I heard we were getting an intern.

As small business owners and managers know, there is a lot to do around the office. With limited staff, there's never enough time in the business day (or regular day) to get everything accomplished. An intern can be a valuable, and inexpensive, asset.

I gleefully pranced into my boss's office and asked if the rumor was true. My boss confirmed it. Before I closed the door behind me, I already had a mental list of all the (ahem) "jobs" my intern could do. It wasn't hard for me to come up with a list that looked like an errand boy's nightmare. My intern was going to get donuts, do deliveries, typeset trivial stories and file like there was no tomorrow. Just like I did when I was an intern.

I interned for a public relations firm when I was home from college for the summer. While I did get some scrap stories or projects thrown to me, I was always the one to get bagels or drop off a letter clear across town. I hated that part of the job. I wanted the chance to prove myself, but instead, my biggest responsibility was making sure I got fat-free and regular cream cheese on my bagel runs. Had to have them both, you know.

I can't believe I was about to put my intern through that ordeal. I reconsidered my thoughts and realized how lucky we were to have extra help. Interns are like sponges and want to learn about whatever business you run. It's important to give them the chance. The trick, though, is finding one.

Here are some suggestions to help the search:

First things first. Make sure you write down the intern's job requirements. Do it as if you were looking for a new employee. List the job requirements and the experience the intern would gain. It makes the later steps easier if you're prepared. Then list it in the local paper.

Contact schools. Local high schools and college's have a great pool of interested students. Depending on your business, you may have to stick with just college students because of age or experience requirements.

Train and track. Once you receive inquiries, get resumes and go through the hiring process as you would any job seeker. Once an intern is hired, train them and adhere to your list of job requirements. Take the time to get to know them, too. Even if your intern moves on, they'll talk about their time with your business and may refer a potential client.

Use your intern like you would an employee and you'll be surprised at how valuable they can become. Who knows? You may be grooming your perfect employee, too.

Keeping children happy at work is nothing more than child's play

I had an expensive paperweight, given to me by a close friend. It sat on the end of my desk like a good luck piece. It was late Monday; I was tired and ready to go home and working like mad to get a story written for our newsletter. I thought I saw something move and quickly looked up. My paperweight was missing! I couldn't stop my work to look for it, so I kept pecking away at the keyboard.

Moments later I stopped for a break and looked up. My paperweight was where it was earlier. I leaned back in my chair and rubbed my eyes. I had to be seeing things. I was about to shake it off as a sign of computer fatigue until I heard a muffled giggle.

Instead of getting back to work, I looked in the direction of the paperweight and began to aimlessly type. As I did a small hand reached over the edge of the desk and snatched the paperweight again.

Again the giggle, this time accompanied by a snort.

A giggle and snort? I wasn't suffering from computer fatigue. I was a victim of my boss's child and his little game of hide and seek.

With more and more small businesses becoming flexible and meeting the needs of employees, children are invading the workplace. I even bring in my daughter from time to time. No matter how hard you try to deter them from getting their hands on office equipment, they always find a way.

Here are some tips to make it a little more difficult:

Reach for an answer. Put all your valuable items, like expensive paperweights, out of a child's reach. Move computers, keyboards and anything else that can break easily to higher ground and out of reach.

Make space. When children get into the office, they want to be part of the work. Sit them at an empty desk and let them write on a pad and paper. Give them a pretend assignment. Children love to act like adults, so let them.

Lock 'em if you have 'em. If you have locks on drawers turn the key and keep the children out for good. It's the easiest way to keep hands away from sensitive material, young or otherwise.

I eventually caught my paperweight thief and tortured him with a tickle until he promised never to do it again. It was a nice break and I finished my writing shortly thereafter. But some employees aren't as eager to play with children and that is their right. Let children know what they can and can't do when they get into the office.

Once you figure that out and they listen, everything else is child's play.

Seating arrangements should be taken seriously

Somewhere in my job description, buried under the fictional title of box mover and light bulb changer, is table mover. How it fits under director of publications is anyone's guess, but it's there.

My office hosts several functions in our large boardroom and we need volunteers to set up tables in different configurations to accommodate our guests. It's not my favorite thing to do, not even close. It's for the better of the organizations, though, so I always pitch in.

I'm getting good at it, too. A few co-workers and myself can arrange the room in a variety of patterns in just a few minutes. We know the half-moon, the classroom, the box and u-shapes like a football player's play book. Each set is for a particular event.

It's the bizarre, off-centered arrangements that get the most attention, even though they are rarely used. Some of the more creative ones are the infamous plus or x-shape and the T-shape, like in a James Bond movie. If criminal masterminds can decide they want to rule the world in this configuration, why can't small business owners?

And I can't forget to mention the Chaotic Configuration of Doom. It can't be overlooked. It's too famous. Just throw the tables in random order and then sit back and watch an executive look for the head of the table to sit. I'm holding that one until I really, really need it.

Preparing for a meeting is a tricky business. Everything from trash locations to table arrangements is critical if you're hosting potential clients or other professionals.

Here are some tips:

Sit down. The best seating-arrangement shapes, although not the most creative, are the circle (or square), the u-shape or one big rectangle. People can identify the front of the room and sit accordingly. It's also the most recognizable and will make people feel comfortable.

Hear this. Make sure everyone can hear everyone else. We use a microphone in our conference room, so this isn't a problem. However, without a microphone it can be a challenge depending on the room's size. Test your voice before deciding on a room's arrangement.

Chatroom. If you have any control of where people sit, use it to your advantage. Don't put antagonists near each other or face-to-face. Put talkative people, or potential troublemakers, near the speaker to keep some sort of control.

I'd write more, but the conference room needs me. More tables to set up, you know. It appears we might have a group of potential rabble-rousers coming in. I get to try out my latest seating arrangement. It's called the blockade. We'll pile up all the tables in front of the doors and see if the group can get in.

Of course, I won't be able to get out.

Which may not be a bad idea if the seating arrangement doesn't work.

Dress code mystery explored

I'm going to try and crack that Friday folly small businesses like to call the dress code. I tried my best to track down those blue jeans buffers and those ruffled-shirt rules to find out exactly what a dress code is and why it's so vague sometimes.

No one gave me a straight answer during my individual search and the Internet turned up nothing. I had to bring in my own people.

I don't know if the powers-that-be were trying to pull a fast one or if they were nothing more than cool-cucumbers in this big refrigerator full of business. Dress slacks and silk ties beware, the code is out there. If it can be broken, my fashion fighters will find a way. Here's what some of my best code breakers said:

Hoops McGee, super-investigating reporter and part-time fashion consultant for the hotel valet industry. Hoops, what's the deal with dress codes?

They typically happen on a Friday when not too much happens at the office. Depending on the particular code in question, casual dress can range from shorts and t-shirts to dress slacks and collared shirts.

Did you break the code, Hoops?

No. It's a tough one to crack.

Minnie Goodpants, runner-up to thirty-six consecutive first round "Millionaire" trivia contestants and expert Barbie doll dresser. How often are these codes enforced?

Sometimes they are strictly enforced, other times they

aren't. Every business should enforce its dress code. Studies indicate those who abide by the rules are disgruntled when they see an employee get away with the slightest deviation.

Why have codes at all?

For the most part it's good mojo, or karma. It's the bad apples that spoil the bunch.

The code, Minnie, did you break it?

Not yet. It's heavily encrypted.

Rotten code. Maybe Bongo Marie, native woodcutter from Eaton Rapids and fashion editor for the now defunct and out of print "Sewer Styles" magazine, has the answer.

Bongo, how popular are these dress codes?

They are very popular. Employers have to look for creative ways to keep employees happy. One of those is relaxing the office rules a bit and letting them dress down on certain days. It's that good mojo thing Minnie mentioned.

What about rules?

Employers need to make clear what is acceptable. If you leave it up to a vague description and leave it open to interpretation, you'll have various shades of casual. Pick one and stick with it.

That sound's about right. Did you crack the code?

No. But I found a cute pair of slacks.

Not the same thing, Bongo. At least we learned more about the crafty code of the dress. From casual, ultra-casual to downright roll-out-of-bed pajamas, dress codes are different and need to be enforced.

If everyone did that, then the code would be broken and my plumber-crack outfit will have to find different work.

Creative perks in the workplace make for happy employees

Small business owners often find themselves at the mercy of big business when battling for quality employees. That's why creative perks are more important than ever.

Every small business owner knows hiring employees with potential and keeping him or her around in today's market isn't easy. Small business owners can't compete with salary and big-time benefits like full medical, dental and vision coverage or extended vacation time — the heavy artillery of big business benefits.

Losing out to a big business that can provide such luxury perks can mean frustration to small business owners who have spent a lot time and money for the employee. Not to mention the headache in starting the process all over again from scratch.

However, all is not lost. Put away that white flag and listen up soldier! Creative perks are becoming the answer to the employee war. Finding alternative ways to keep an employee happy, besides lining their wallet with money, is sometimes the only way a small business can compete on equal footing with big business. Creative doesn't mean costly either. Talk to employees and ask them what they might consider as perks and look into it. You'd be surprised at what makes them tick.

But, before you do, check out my list. It may give you ideas.

In the office. Bring your pet to work day, daycare, education classes, financial planning service, personal expense account, legal service, massages, parking privileges, and telecommuting.

Out of the office. Service to pick up pets, take vehicles for service, dry cleaning service, elderly care, gym time, handyman services for home repairs, laundry service, magazine subscriptions, recreation programs (softball, bowling leagues, etc.) and scholarships.

Might cost a bit. Alternative medical care (chiropractic, herbal remedies, etc.), discounts at area restaurants or theaters, extra vacation time, memberships in trade or professional association, event tickets (sports, opera, rock concerts, home improvement, etc.), trips to a getaway destination or zero percent loans.

Answer the phone in a human voice; computers take away the service edge

It was supposed to be a routine call. Dial the number, place an order, give a pleasantry or two and hang up. Simple directions for a simple task. Better yet, it was the exact process I normally take to order something from a small business. But this wasn't a small business I was calling. It was a big business.

But they can't be much different, right?

I needed to order software for my computer from a national catalogue warehouse. After letting the phone ring five times, I should have hung up, but someone on the other end picked up. A cold, computerized voice crackled appreciation for my call and put me through a maze of extensions and time wasting options. My patience wore thin.

All I wanted was a simple software update for my computer.

The company was the only one selling the product I needed so I had to trudge my way through the call. After three or four minutes of jumping through hoops, listening to painfully slow music that isn't fit for elevators, I finally talked to a human. Once I got to the operator, the call breezed by. Go figure. I looked at my watch. Fifteen minutes of my life was wasted.

Unless it's a huge order, there is no way a phone call should take that long. Most times it doesn't, especially when dealing with a small business. With fewer employees, fewer phone lines and more personality than a big business can put on hold, small businesses have the power to keep a customer interested and satisfied on the phone.

Here are some sure-fire phone tips that can help win the phone service race:

For whom the phone rings. Answer the phone on the second or third ring. It shows you're ready for action. Always respond in a courteous tone and don't make a lot of small talk unless the customer initiates it. This keeps the length of the call down.

Use the phrase that pays. It helps to have a small sheet of paper next to each phone with frequently asked business questions for new employees. Every small business owner, who has been in business for a long time, can recite a long list of commonly asked questions. Pick the best and share the knowledge with your staff.

Be busy, very busy. Whether you're busy or not, it pays to act like it. If the customer is trying to set up an appointment let them know you could fit them in at 10 a.m. That way your customer will think you're in high demand and taking time out to really service them.

Simple pleasantries and direct conversation make routine phone calls enjoyable, informative, productive and well ... routine.

Take control of your finances before someone does it for you

Employee theft isn't fun for anyone. It's hard to imagine a trusted employee pillaging the petty cash, emptying the cash register or forging company checks, but it happens.

At a recent seminar, I sat with other association executives at a large table. We were learning about financing and the topic shifted to employee theft. It was like turning on a light inside a haunted house to these staff members as they let the stories fly. Each story more traumatic than the other.

I felt like I was at a meeting with Stephen King, Wes Craven and Alfred Hitchcock. The stories were so scary. I didn't want to look at the walls because I thought they would start to bleed. I wanted to tell them to turn off the light and end the meeting, but it was too late. The told the stories anyway.

One woman told of how she first started her job. She walked in and looked at the $500 sitting in her petty cash. Knowing that was too much, she remarked out loud and in front of her employees to take some of the money and put it in the bank. The next day someone did. The woman came into work and the $500 was missing. The bank didn't know where it went, and surprise, neither did the employees.

The table let out a gasp. I think Hitchcock smiled.

Another executive chimed in about an elaborate scam between her CEO and bookkeeper. This dishonest pair embezzled money from the association. In order to cover their tracks, the bookkeeper opened the mail first, took out the return checks, forged the bank statement and approved it. That went on for 10 years.

We just shook our head in disbelief. Craven and King gave each other a high five.

Don't think it won't happen to you. Small business owners wear plenty of hats to ensure their success, but at the same time, so do your employees. Trust is good, but so is common sense.

The following control checks can curb employee theft:

Sign language. If the treasurer or check signer is also the bookkeeper, two signatures should be required on all checks. It should be a policy. A law. A way of life in your business.

Log it. A person other than the bookkeeper should receive bank statements from the bank and should record them. Experts suggest someone that doesn't have check signing authority do this. A lot of times it falls into the lap of the receptionist.

Use receipts. Receipts are like gold. Use them for petty cash. Make sure you know exactly where every penny from your business is spent. Deposit your other receipts in the bank, intact and on a timely basis. It keeps your records current and moves large amounts of money from your store and to a safe area.

These are just a few examples of controls. There are many other ideas a certified public account can give you. Explore them if you think you may be a victim of employee theft.

If nothing else it will let you sleep easier at night and keep the boogey man away.

Part Six:
Marketing

Marketing is connected to higher sales. Higher sales are connected to more profits. More profit is connected to a bigger smile on the face of a small business owner. The bigger the smile, the better the chance the small business owner won't stay small for long. Hey, even Microsoft started small. Use these tips and you may be next to make it big. Just remember your old pal Tim when you do.

Business cards: Carry them and use them often

How does a small business owner in the tiny town of Crystal, Michigan, who sells used industrial uniforms, get a nationwide client list?

Take a guess.

A well-funded advertising campaign, you say?

Nope.

How about telemarketing?

Nope.

The Internet?

Good guess, but no.

This small business owner mastered an effective campaign of passing out his business card to anyone who would accept it. I even got a few of them in my pocket by the time I finished the interview.

His business card isn't traditional in any sense, which adds another wrinkle to this tale. It's a roughly shaped rectangle cut from a regular sheet of paper. A laser printer didn't print the card judging by the font's tired, worn look, lending itself to the simple side of efficient.

Not a great deal of expense went into these cards, but, boy, are they effective.

He swears by them and judging by his success, he's on to something. Anytime he takes a trip he stuffs his pockets and makes sure to visit places that would likely use reconditioned uniforms: gas stations, truck stops and every bulletin board he sees on his trip.

Sometimes he sees immediate results. Other times all he has

to do is wait a few weeks and he receives calls at any time of the day. Your small business can see these kinds of results if you follow a few simple rules when it comes to passing out your calling card:

Get it right. Before you even think about passing out your business card, make sure all the information is correct and updated. Nothing looks more unprofessional than passing out cards with an old phone number crossed out and a new one scribbled in its place.

Know the ropes. Like the Crystal business owner, it pays to know where clients lurk. If you sell books, leave your cards at library bulletin boards or kiosks. If you provide a laundry service, try pools or restaurants. As the business owner you should know your clients' demographics and use that to your strength.

Be generous. Mail those cards out in everything that leaves your office. Pass cards to everyone you know. Drop them in fishbowl contests at restaurants. The more you have out, the better chance of a response.

They say a picture is worth a thousand words.

I'll bet a good business card campaign is worth much more.

Positive word of mouth does wonders

A small business needs a positive image. Whether it's dealing with customers or just the community in general, every entrepreneur knows the value of a good reputation.

Unfortunately it takes a lot of hard work to get a good reputation, and only a few harsh words from an unsatisfied customer, an underhanded competitor or a disgruntled employee to tear it away.

I had to deal with an upset employee once, and it was a real experience. We terminated the former employee because of a sub-standard work performance. As a salesman, he didn't meet his quota and it was time for him to move on.

We went separate ways and didn't hear from him for some time. That was until he took a job at a competing business, selling not only to our clients, but spreading rumors about my business. We saw a lack of sales and heard reports that many of the small town's residents were beginning to doubt we were a reputable. We managed to nip the problem in the bud with a positive public relations campaign to increase our customer service and spent several hours after contributing to community service.

The negative rumors quickly subsided and our sales increased.

Here are some other ways to combat negative word-of-mouth:

Change for the better. Like my business, it pays to hear what people are saying and to address the problem. Sometimes it could be a simple solution. Whatever the case, though, do your best to correct it.

Watch your customers. Despite my tale, unhappy clients usually spread negative comments. If you hear one, there may be others. Compile your complaints and see if there's a pattern. It could be very revealing.

Plan ahead. It's easy to get complacent when things go well. Take the time to sit down and look at areas that need improving and design a plan in case of bad publicity. It will soften the blow and make your business look very professional.

It's good to be ready for a problem, but all the planning in the world can't make you ready for everything. Just make sure to focus on the positives, it will eventually work — you have my word on that.

Set your sights on business goals; make the right contacts

Before entering the work force many years ago, my college professors gave me a piece of advice. They told me it's not what you know, it's whom you know that will make all the difference in the business world. A great piece of advice for anyone in business.

I was eager to tell my professors all about my list of who's who in the business world when I went to speak at my alma mater. I had to wait through the whole job career program before I had the chance to get my professors together in one place. I wanted their attention at the same time because my list was impressive. I wrote all the names on a piece of paper because I didn't want to forget anyone I had conversed with or that helped me out.

My English professor heard about my list (I had been doing a little bragging with some of my former classmates) and caught me off guard in front of the group.

"Are those your contacts, Tim?"

I should have held up the list, displaying it proudly to everyone in the group. I should have said "yes, sir!" I should have done a victory dance while chanting the names. But I didn't do anything.

Instead, I looked at my shoulders and my sport coat and dropped to my knees looking for my contacts.

"Did they fall out again?" I asked. Everyone laughed.

My list became smaller and smaller in my hands. While contacts are important for your vision, know the difference and, in some cases, be ready to show who you know. Here are ways to improve your contacts:

Call 'em. If you're like most small business people, you'll have a Rolodex full of names and numbers. Make sure to keep that current. Go through it on a regular basis. While you're at it you'll find names and numbers of people you haven't talked to in a long time. Make an effort to call at least three people a day you haven't talked to lately. It's a great way to touch base and renew acquaintances.

Meet 'em. Go to community meetings. Check local newspapers for a calendar of events. Some good meetings to attend are charity events, community gatherings and maybe even your local municipality's regular session.

Speak up. When you attend social events, mingle with the crowd. Bring your business card and pass it out. Don't be afraid to meet new people and to get to know them. It's one thing to make an effort to speak to them, but also make it an effort to listen to what they are saying. You may have the same interests and click.

And if you're ready to show off that list at your alma mater, make sure you wear glasses. At least you know when they fall off your face.

Do you have what it takes to be the company's spokesperson?

When a reporter calls do you have what it takes to step to the microphone and be the company spokesperson? A lot of small business owners think they have the right stuff, but seldom make the most of the opportunity.

A good spokesperson needs to think on the fly, have a good voice and look good on television or in a photo. They need to know how to say facts about their business. They need to sound intelligent and quotable.

Sound hard? It's not really, but it does take practice. Media representatives train for years to sound the way they do so don't be discouraged if your first attempts don't make the inside spread of *Time Magazine*.

Here are some tips for your fifteen seconds of fame:

Call a coach. If you know you have an interview looming in the near future, it may be a good idea to call a person who knows what they are doing. You could call a media specialist at your local college or university to get some tips, or you could hire a communications specialist to help.

Look the part. This is very important, especially when doing television. A bad dress day could look disastrous on film. If you have a picture you'd like to appear in a newspaper, it might be a good idea to put together a press packet with a professional photograph. If the movie stars can do it, you can too.

Break a leg. The best thing you can do before an interview is practice. Be sincere in your response and if you have to script out questions and have a co-worker fire them back to you, do it. It will get you ready for questions that might otherwise catch you off guard. Give your small business the opportunity for exposure.

When the spotlight is on try to shine.

And don't ever forget to smile.

Logos are important to a business' identity

Small or home-based businesses need a logo if they want to succeed. It helps your business achieve a crisp, corporate identity. This is exactly what I told the group of community college students I was lecturing. I talked about the importance of having a small business communications plan. I stressed the significance of coming up with a name for a business and then a logo, but the class must have misunderstood.

A bombardment of questions followed my hour-long speech.

"Uh, Mr. Kissman, I can't see a logo being that important."

Would McDonald's be the same without the Golden Arches? Would the Olympics be the same with connected squares instead of rings? Or what about Macintosh computers without their trademark apple? Logos are crucial to identity and should be the most important things your business creates.

"Yeah, but aren't they hard to create? I mean you have to be very skilled to come up with a logo."

No, you don't. A logo can be a simple as a letter or shape. There are virtually hundreds of different software options on the market to help you design a logo. All you need is imagination, creativity and patience. Some of the best logos ever are also the simplest. Think about Visa and MasterCard or Coke and Pepsi. These are huge companies who started small at one time and people have come to identify their product simply by their logo.

If that doesn't work, there are graphic designers and art majors that live for the chance to design a logo. Check with your local college or call around to small businesses that have logos you like and find out who they used.

"What do you do with a logo?"

A better question is what don't you do with one? Put that logo on anything that goes out of your office. Use it on stationary, envelopes, folders, mailing labels, invoices or fax cover pages. Put it on the side of your building or in every advertisement you can muster. That logo will be your identity. If it's good and used effectively, people will associate your logo with your business. It will communicate the nonverbal image you want your company to convey.

My answers seemed to tame the students' curiosity and hopefully provided them with the information they needed to take the next step. Logos are important to a business and with careful planning and management, they could propel a business to the next level.

I stake my name, and logo, on it.

107

Selling gift certificates can increase your business traffic

Trying to pick the perfect gift for a family member or close friend is never easy, especially if the gift is for that seldom-seen relative who already owns everything under the sun.

My personal experience is nothing to brag about. I wish I had a simple answer to find the perfect gift, but I don't. I've scoured store after store looking for the knick-knack or gadget no one on this Earth could possibly possess, but have always come up empty. Or with something the relative already owns. He's polite about receiving it and feigns a surprise, but I bet he either gives it away or simply returns it for something he needs.

After years of rising to the challenge of finding a gift, I shifted gears and bought a gift certificate every time a holiday or birthday came up. The businesses that offer gift certificate get my business, the ones that don't — they see me walk by their door. Gift certificates are great marketing tools and if done correctly, they can become a great resource to bring customers back after their initial visit.

Here are some ideas to protect your business from gift certificate fraud:

Customize it. If you buy generic gift certificates from a stationary or office supply store you're inviting trouble. If you can find them so can a thief. Make sure you make or purchase unique ones. Use an imbedded watermark or embossed logo, too. The more original, the less likely it is for someone to come up with a duplication.

Log it. When you issue one of your customized certificates, record it. Record the certificate number, the date of sale and the dollar amount. If possible, record who is buying it. Match the certificate with your records when redeemed.

Cash out. Avoid cash refunds. You want your customers to use the certificate to move merchandise, not drain your cash register. An easy way to ensure this is to state on the certificate if more than five dollars of change is due you will issue another certificate. Major chains do this. It protects you from someone buying a pack of gum on a $50 certificate, and brings the customer back into your store.

These are simple ways to make gift certificates safe and manageable for your business. It also gives you the chance to say you have something for everyone.

Even long lost relatives.

Never judge a book by its cover

When it comes to direct mail, there are two types of letters that find their way to the desk of prospective clients or business contacts. There are the chosen few opened and actually read, and there are the ones that are immediately tossed into the trash. What separate the trash from the cash? Many people look at the return address to see who sent it. Others, look for a stamp or a metered mark.

The trick in the small business, direct-marketing scheme of getting people to read your mail is to rid the letter world of prejudice and grab your intended recipient's attention with a letter that looks personal.

Every business has a strategy, no matter how faulty, when it comes to direct mail. The successful research mailing lists and spend their advertising budget wisely. Businesses that don't do research wind up scratching their heads, trying to figure out why more people don't come to their grand opening.

Some small business owners don't have the luxury of a staff, so they need to be creative in their own way. It's unfortunate, but time and budget can limit creativity. Don't use that excuse and let your mail fall through the cracks.

Read my tips, then get out there and so some research:

Give it personality. Try to get the name of the person you are targeting with your mailing, not just his or her title. People open mail addressed to them. Mail addressed to occupant, manager or resident finds its way to the trash.

Be closed minded. Window envelopes look like a solicitation or a bill. No one wants to open those. Instead, send your direct mail in a clean white business envelope. Hand address it if you can. Make it look like a personal letter and it might get a little more attention than normal. If you're daring, take it one step farther by using a small return address that doesn't reveal the name of the business.

Stamp of approval. The sure-fire way of getting people to open your letter is to lose the meter and give it a stamp. While it may be costly with larger mailings, it does look more personal. Another option might be to use a third class pre-sorted stamp, which carries the bulk rate, but looks like a regular stamp.

It doesn't matter what the letter says — the simple fact remains potential clients don't take the time to open bulk mail unless it interests them. Devise a plan for your direct mail and follow it no matter how much extra time it takes.

In other words, follow every detail, right down to the letter.

Pass out the freebies and watch the clients come

If you take a look at my desk, you'd be surprised at what you find.

Behind the empty wrappers of gum, pieces of scrap paper that make up my graveyard of lost telephone numbers and pen caps chewed beyond recognition is a museum of freebies I've received from vendors. Coffee mugs are plentiful and so are my free "to do" lists and scratch pads of paper. I can't work without my squishy ball and my paperweight — well, if I could open my window I'm sure a breeze would blow my work of the desk, so I need that paperweight.

I don't use all my freebies all the time, but when I do, I look at the name of the person who gave it to me. I may even think about why I have the freebie at all. Freebies give businesses an advantage over competition. It's an effective way to get your business's message out and increase your chance of getting a repeat visit from your customer. It works on me.

Buy hey, if you don't believe me, here's what the marketing experts say:

Give it away. Giving away freebies can and does lead to increased traffic flow to your business. Having those freebies, with your logo and message, all over an office or public area can only help sales. Sounds like the top goals for a pricey advertising campaign, doesn't it? See my squishy ball?

Pick a budget. If you're thinking about giving away freebies, first decide on how much you'd like to spend on a gift and what you want to give. Try to tie it as closely to your business as possible. Once you have that figured out, ask yourself about the message and include a logo. Did I mention I received a barbecue set, too?

Pass them out. Give freebies to as many people or businesses as possible. It's great to have the freebie, but if it sits on your shelf, then it isn't worth the investment. Pass them out at parades or other community events and make sure every customer you deal with has one. T-shirts are nice, too. I wear a XXLT.

Whoever said the best things in life are free was right — they are, especially when they have your company's name, address and telephone number on them.

Contests can make your business ideas into winners

Don't you just love a good contest?

My co-workers love them. I do too. It's what makes everyone tick and the allure of winning big can't be denied.

For the past several years my office has held friendly games for our office holiday party. The first year we went on a treasure hunt, venturing outside to find a variety of clues on a windy, and cold, mid-Michigan December afternoon. When the contest ended and everyone's toes thawed out, you should have heard the stories. Everyone loved it. The same people who loved to be in the warmth of the office and always complained about the cold, forgot where they were and became competitors, braving sub-zero temperatures to find the next clue in a treasure hunt.

It was great to watch. I, of course, was on the committee who planned the event and stayed inside where it was warm. It pays to be the creative one in the office.

As a small business owner, running a contest could be a great way to generate some business and additional interest in your company. If my co-workers can get that excited, I can only imagine what a client would do if there was a worthy prize on the line.

While large companies do it on a grand scale, there are some great contests that smaller companies can do on a tight budget. It could take some time, but with creativity and the right marketing plan, you could get valuable information, name recognition, publicity, goodwill and employee pride.

Sounds good doesn't it? Here's what to consider:

Plan it. Any good contest must reach an objective. If you want to increase your database information, then a simple give-away raffle would work. If you're looking to get people in your store, a multiple-purchase card could be the answer. Pay attention to what works for other stores and see if it fits into your scheme. But have an objective before you start.

Be the expert. Keep the contest within your genre. For example, if you're a bookstore, you could sponsor an essay contest with high school kids and give out a book. If you're a restaurant, give away a free meal to an aspiring chef. Good contests that generate entries don't have to have deep pockets. You can really establish yourself within the community when you try to educate or encourage youth or someone's talent.

Smile. Everyone loves a winner. Whether it's a hotdog eating contest or a treasure hunt, people become interested. Many times it's the contest, not the prize, that will drive people to your business. Once it's over play up the winner like he or she is an Olympic gold medal winner. Snap pictures, send out a press release and see what happens.

It's rewarding to plan the contest, too, and to see it unfold before your eyes. Of course the sound of your cash register filling up is just as nice.

And that's a prize every small businessperson wants to win.

When you need a quick solution put a classified ad on the case

WANTED: BRIEFCASE SNATCHER (S) RESPONSIBLE FOR PICKING UP BROWN LEATHER BRIEFCASE FROM STREET SECONDS BEFORE OWNER COULD CLAIM IT. CONTENTS MOST IMPORTANT, BUT WOULD LIKE BOTH BACK A.S.A.P. FOR REWARD CALL TIM KISSMAN AT ....

Finding my briefcase is going to be as hard as finding quality employees. I've exhausted every avenue. I've called lost and founds, police stations and even parking attendants and valets, but no one knows where it is. I only have one recourse left: the classifieds.

I left my parking ramp with the bag perched on the top of my car. You see I put it on the roof of my car so I could climb around the passenger side door. The driver side door always sticks. I usually remember the briefcase and yank it in before I pull away. On this day, however, it got the ride of its life.

As you can probably guess, I turned a corner and it flew off the roof. I managed to pull the car over a few hundred feet away (it's hard to stop on one way streets) and by the time I ran back to the briefcase, it was gone.

I'm most upset someone beat me to my briefcase like it was some sort of prize duck swimming at a county fair midway booth. All the winner had to do was be the first to pluck it out of the concrete river and it was his. Those darn pluckers.

But as I sat in my car, defeated and miffed, I began to realize what I lost. Not only did I lose a nice gift from my wife, but several valuable documents, including my first manuscript. None of which I'll ever see again.

I thought about setting up a roadblock and searching everyone's car but the police suggested I try the ad instead. In retrospect it's probably the wiser choice.

Will the pen prove mightier than the patrol car and my sure-proof roadblocks? I hope so. Here are some tips when writing a classified ad:

Size does matter. Keep classified ads short and to the point. Try to tell as much as you can in as few words as you can. If you're worried about losing the meaning have someone else read it and see if they understand.

Make an impact. Chose active, interesting words to keep the reader's attention. Words like "free," "exciting" and "wanted" are perfect and spur interest. Check the spelling, and double check the ad. It helps to keep a copy of your draft, in case the paper makes a mistake.

Let them know. Make it easy for the reader to know why

they should contact you or what action they should take. Provide phone numbers and contact names. The easier it is for them to get a hold of you, the greater the chance you'll have that they'll call.

Part Seven:
'Tis the Seasonal Tips and Keeping Stress to a Minimum

Think the holidays are just a once-a-year event? Hardly. When the holiday season comes around, small businesses do whatever they can to spread goodwill. If that kind of effort were applied to a year round effort, just think of how many clients and business friends you'd have. I can guarantee you wouldn't feel stressed or sick because Santa would be sliding down your chimney in January, February, March ... you get the picture.

Pick a card, any card, to let business relationships know you care

If there was ever a time of the year more perfectly suited toward building business relationships than the holiday season, I'd like to see it. The holiday season is a great opportunity to let clients know you appreciate their relationship. Every business I've conducted business with decorates its walls with the holiday greeting cards they get in the mail. To a new customer it can't help but look good to walk into an office and see the cards from other associates.

It doesn't have to be a big ordeal to select them, either. Just make sure you get a personal message across while expressing happy holidays or another generic holiday greeting. That's really important. Picking a Merry Christmas card may be appropriate to you, but it may offend clients that aren't celebrating the holiday because of religious beliefs. It also gives you leeway to send season's greetings' cards until the first week of January. Not a bad little trick, eh?

Some business owners design their own cards, adding an extra personal touch. But it doesn't have to be so complicated. Holiday cards range from businesses simply getting all their employees to sign the inside of a blank card to companies who hire artists to do caricatures of their employees.

Here are some other good holiday card-giving tips:

Make a list, check it twice. Be sure your holiday card list is complete. If you send a holiday card to one client, while forgetting another, it may reflect poorly on your business. It's good to have another employee check out the list and make sure you didn't forget anybody.

Give 'em a hand. Don't use a computer or buy a card that's already done. It isn't as personal as writing a message by hand. It may take a few extra minutes, but the reward is worth it. Just make sure you have good handwriting, though.

Send the cards out early. That's simple. The U.S. Postal Service is swamped with holiday well-wishers at the last minute. The closer to Christmas, the less chance your cards have of making it on time. If you're stuck in a crunch and need to get some sort of greeting out, online services offer electronic greeting cards. It's not the same as getting a card in the mail, but they do have some interesting cards. These cards come complete with animation and music, but no handwriting.

The holiday season comes only once a year. It's good to plan ahead and make sure you have the clients you want to build a good relationship on your card list, especially if you want to play in their reindeer games once the season is over.

Besides, no one likes to be a Grinch.

Having a party? Take your time and plan it right

Hosting parties for your small business can be a great way to increase visibility, meet new customers and show good will toward your local community. It doesn't matter what the occasion, either.

Traditional reasons for a party can be a grand opening, remodeling and reaching a sales goal or a retirement. Non-traditional reasons, like 'just because' are also common. I like those the best.

But that doesn't have to be the limit. Have a party to welcome a new business. Why not host an event during a national holiday? Or better yet, celebrate your birthday – it's your business, have fun with it.

Before you plan your next event, entertain these ideas for making it a success:

Make a date. Check the calendar before making a party date. Avoid major holidays or sporting events. No matter how well you plan an event, people won't come if it falls on the same night as the NCAA Final Four.

Plan everything. Make sure you list everything you need. The easy items to remember are food and refreshments, but what about chairs and an adequate number of waste cans? I hate going to parties where I have to leave my plate on the table or go on a search for a trash can. Do a quick run through before your guests arrive. You may be surprised at what you find.

Are you kidding? Let guests know if children are welcomed. If you deal in antiques or other collectibles and have the party inside your business it may be a good idea to limit partygoers to adults. If kids are welcomed make sure there's entertainment because I'd hate to see what happens when a child gets curious with your $2,000 computer.

Invite people who can help or have helped your business and follow a theme. These are just a few ways to add punch to your gala.

Oh yeah, one more thing, don't forget to invite me.

Where your donations should go during the giving season

When the holiday season nears, small businesses need to think about shopping for presents, receiving presents, eating pounds of turkey and making a company donation. The holiday season always seems to make small business owners and employees think about the less fortunate. It's wonderful to see everyone rally around a cause.

Sometimes, though, small businesses have trouble deciding which cause to support. Charities compete for the limited resources handed out every year by businesses and making the right choice can be a difficult decision. If you're like me, you want to donate to all of them.

Making a list and checking it twice doesn't cut it all the time. I've been involved with countless discussions to donate holiday money. We've discussed giving it to a local family or a local charitable organization, and one time we gave it all to an individual who needed it most. It isn't an easy decision to make especially when the money or gift comes from everyone in the office. People have different beliefs and finding a cause that can suit them all can be difficult.

But Rudolph, with his nose so bright, didn't give up on Christmas Eve and neither should a small business when it comes to donating. Here are some ideas and items to consider when trying to choose a charity:

Write it out. Charities should provide written information to your business on how the group intends to use your company's donations. Check out how much of each dollar goes to true charitable purposes.

Know this. Be aware of organizations with high-pressure calls or mail solicitations. Avoid charities that don't or won't send written material until you donate money. Insist on using the mail, too. Don't let someone pick up your donation. Don't ever donate cash, either.

Take time. If all else fails and you can't decide on where to donate your money, try donating time or services instead. Charities love volunteers and you may have a whole office full of potential candidates. As the owner, you could be really generous and allow employees to use company time to help the charity. I bet it makes your participation higher.

The holiday season is a great for giving. Make it a good investment by taking a few precautions. And best of all, make someone's holiday by giving.

Decorating windows can be a pain in the glass

Since every other small business in town decorated its windows, my boss decided to get in the holiday spirit, too. She loved the holidays and wanted to tell the world she was the merriest in town. Unfortunately for my co-workers and I it meant extra duty for a while. Besides our regular day-to-day activities, we had decorating the office jammed to the top of our priority list. It didn't matter if we were naughty or nice – everyone had to pitch in.

In a day, we were to get out last year's ornaments, clean the front reception area, decorate the windows and be merrier than ever. With smiles on our faces we tackled our jobs with holiday zeal. After fighting our way through cluttered ornament boxes and trying to straighten out a tangled, snarled ball of lights while taking subscription orders over the phone, we were ready for the holidays to end. It didn't help the only holiday tape to keep us in the mood was the *Chipmunks Greatest Hits.*

We made it through that day and our office never looked better. It wasn't solely because of the ornaments, either. Every time we tacked something to the wall, or strung it over a counter, we cleaned the surface first. It's amazing how much dust and dirt can collect during the year – especially when the furnaces come to life in the cold weather.

Keep these tips in mind when you're decorating your office (keep it clean year round and you may not need these):

Delegate. If you have an even number of staff members, or at least more than two, delegate the cleaning and decorating duties. Ornaments can be dusty and so can the places where you want to put them. It's easier to have one person in charge of washing and another hanging. Think assembly line. It works for Santa's elves.

Less is more. The best decorated houses and businesses are the ones who do a tasteful job of decorating. They use the same-colored lights and a modest amount of other decorations. Don't use a string of white lights here, a string of colored ones there, and a dancing Santa on every available surface. It doesn't look good on my neighbor's house and certainly won't for your business.

Stow it, carefully. Learn from last year's mistakes and take the time to put away the ornaments neatly. It's easy to remember the ornaments when the Christmas spirit is everywhere, but when you're ready to take them down (and please do it sometime in the early part of January, my neighbor leaves his up year 'round) put them in storage boxes. Take the time to unravel the lights and roll them up. It'll save time later.

Our office was a success. Visitors from all over to town came to the office to view our decorations and spend some time chatting. It also helped to have some candy canes to pass out and some warm cider at the ready.

Happy holidays and good luck decorating.

Here's a Christmas jingle about annoying e-mails

On the first day of last week, someone e-mailed to me ... a story about Bill Gates sending $100 to everybody.

This particular e-mail said Gates is testing tracking software that sends $100 to everyone who forwards it to at least 10 other people. Yeah, right. It's nothing more than a stupid scam. E-mail scams and spamming are an epidemic on the Internet. It's hopeless thinking everyone who has an e-mail address can use it responsibly, but maybe they can see a scam, or urban legend, for what it is and delete it if they get one.

But they don't and for some reason I'm on their e-mail list. I'm not on anyone's list for one big computer virus, but my name pops up for useless messages throughout the year. To them I say thanks. You've inspired me to compose this holiday song.

On the second day of last week, someone e-mailed to me ... a tale about free gift certificates from Old Navy, and Cracker Barrel, or Victoria's Secret.

Again, it's the old forward the e-mail scam. E-coupons don't work like that and there is no way a company would pay people to forward e-mail, like this scam promises. The more e-mails, the greater the discount. Think about it, there are millions and millions of e-mail users out there and a company would wind up losing a great deal of money. So quit forwarding the e-mails and clogging up people's inboxes!

I know, I know ... on with the song.

On the third day of last week, someone e-mailed to me... a ludicrous needle at the gas pump story.

This e-mail comes from Florida. It's a warning to unsuspecting travelers hidden AIDS-infected needles on gas pump handles. This is a doozy of an urban legend. Don't believe it. Leave it up to people in Florida to come up with a story about poking holes in something.

On the fourth day of last week, someone e-mailed to me... at least one of a dozen sob stories.

Everything from little girls dying with cancer, small boys struck by cars and ruthless kidney thieves exist in cyberspace. The message tells a sad story and that someone, somewhere is paying money for every forwarded e-mail. It's impossible to track e-mail. The stories are sad urban legends and it's unfortunate someone thinks they are funny enough to start a scam.

On the fifth day of last week, I turned my computer off.

I couldn't take it anymore.

125

Getting hoax e-mails is something we have to put up with because people love to forward them. It's true; some are very imaginative and make you think, but they aren't real. For more information about Internet scams and hoaxes, check out *www.scambusters.com.* It's a great site and does a wonderful job of debunking a lot of the messages on the Internet.

Handling winter blues means taking care of stress on the job

No matter what small business you run, pressure exists. Every small business owner has to deal with the stress of day-to-day operations, only to have the pressure magnify during the winter months. After the holidays the office slows down, employees return to work, usually with all their vacation time dried up, and settle in until spring.

The sun sets before 5 p.m., but you can't really tell because it's dark and gray outside all day, anyway. Add that to the freezing temperatures that blast your face while you walk to your car every morning and the winds that kick up at night on your way home, and you have a great recipe for the winter blues.

Every person that lives in Michigan has experienced a case of the winter blues in one form or another. It's going to be there so be ready. Whether you have it, or one of your employees, the depression will set in making office life a little more pressure-filled and depressing. It's easy to move piles of work around your desk while saying you'll do it the next day and having a great, big sigh.

Everything in the office that can go wrong does. You need to relax, but nobody ever seems to care. The elevator music, delivered on your desktop radio, used to soothe you, but now you want to throw it into the snow bank.

Relax, take a deep breath and check out these stress-reducing tips:

Make sure to breathe. Sit at your desk, relax your shoulders and take a number of slow, deep breaths. This loosens your muscles and allows your body to have more oxygen. Close your eyes and visualize a place where you'd love to visit. Maybe the beach in Cancun or the streets of Paris. This does wonders. Don't ask me anything for a moment, I'm sipping some fruity drink in my golf cart at Pebble Beach. I'm beating Tiger Woods, too. Isn't imagination wonderful?

Start a hobby. Sitting on your duff all day behind a desk can take its toll. Even though it's dark when you get home, make a point of doing something physical. Clean the house, make some crafts, do aerobics in front of the TV — anything, as long as you move around and expend some energy. Stress builds up during the day and needs a release. Besides it's nice to have a clean house.

Use a screen. If you're at work and can't seem to get anything done because of constant interruptions, screen your calls and make sure you aren't disturbed. Have an employee take messages and return the calls when you're ready to. It's not good to do it all the time, but if you feel you can't handle it during the day, then don't. If you do it once in a while, it's not going to hurt anyone.

These are just a few of the ways you can reduce on-the-job stress. If you want some more ideas, contact your physician. Doctors always have great techniques available. Remember to give yourself an outlet, it makes the winter months much more bearable and spring come that much quicker.

Want to be a weekend warrior? Make sure you can handle it

On most bright, sunny Saturdays it's easy to find me on a golf course. I love hitting the links with the same group of guys I've been golfing with for years.

Lately though, I've been searching for a sub for one of my friends. He's trying to start his own business and the only time he has to work is during the weekends. Saturday mornings for Lee haven't been the same.

It turns out he's not alone. Many full-time business owners started and succeeded by turning their once-relaxed weekends into billable time. Lee's handicap and wallet have inflated since he's undertaken his weekend business, so it's hard to blame him for missing a tee time. But weekend working is taking its toll. He doesn't go out as much, doesn't see his family, and he complains he never gets a break. Working sixty hours a week does that to a person.

He asked me for some advice. I'm the same guy who tried to work on his slice with dreadful advice, but I rose to the challenge. Lee, this one's for you.

Here's how to make the weekend a little more bearable:

Time flies. Make sure you have the time commitment to go ahead with weekend plans. Many fledgling business owners bite off more than they can chew. Working seven days a week can take its toll.

Family ties. Before even thinking about starting a weekend business, check with family members. They can be great support for you when you're working on the weekends. You'll be sacrificing your time with them so make sure it's worth it. It's a good idea to focus on the positive and remind them it may turn into a full-time job.

Saturday = Funday. Remember it's the weekend and it's OK to act like it. Treat yourself to some of the things you liked to do before undertaking a business. If you don't take some breaks here or there, you'll hate the weekends and your great business idea may go up in smoke.

Take time to smell the roses, or in Lee's case the cut grass of the fairway. I reminded him of that early one Saturday morning by pounding on his window. We had a 7 a.m. tee time and I was doing my part as a friend to make sure he followed my advice. Lee didn't quite understand that until he woke up seven holes and six lost golf balls later.

He blamed my golfing advice.

Hey, I tried.

How safe is your home-based business?

Home-based business owners need to make sure their home is safe. Not only for their family, but for the many customers who walk through the door.

My head would definitely thank you.

I recently interviewed a small home-based business owner who re-bound valuable books in his basement. Like many Michigan basements, ceilings and doorways aren't very high and I constantly bent over while taking my nickel tour. Despite my best efforts I bumped my shoulder into a few exposed beams in the wall, scuffed my toe on some of the equipment lying on the floor, and bashed my head against the top of a doorframe.

I'm 6'7" so I'm used to ducking for my life when I'm in public places, but this was ridiculous. Home-based business owners have to pay extra attention to safety details because homeowner's insurance doesn't protect them if a customer slips or hurts himself while in the house.

It's beneficial to think of your customer as one of your

family. Don't let them run with scissors while in the house, play with the stove and best of all, make sure to child proof — er, customer-proof everything in your house.

You just never know.

Here are some tips to prevent an accident and protect you if one occurs.

Policy notes. Check your policy and see exactly what is covered. You may have options to have limited coverage in case of an accident.

Survey the spot. Walk around the office, or any area clients may visit, and make sure it's clear and free of danger. In foul weather, make sure your walk is clear and isn't slippery.

Tell the kids. It's important to let the younger family members know that toys shouldn't be left in the office area. It doesn't look professional and certainly isn't safe. Besides, imagine how embarrassing it would be for a client to go home and tell their spouse they sprained their ankle on a Teletubbie.

It's easy to forget your home is your office. Always remember that it is and do your best to keep it clean and safe for your customers.

Especially the good-looking tall ones.

Education may be your employee's best medicine

During my college basketball days I saw many different types of players. Some were tough, others cowardly and there was always someone who couldn't stay healthy if their life depended on it. So was the case my freshman year. We had a player who would show up to practice and somehow, or someway, injure himself.

In the middle of practice, he'd drop like a sack of potatoes from a twisted ankle. A basketball hit him in the head and he missed the next few practices. He sprained his wrist getting a drink of water and I think his tight shorts made his legs go to sleep for a week.

Looking back at his exploits, I wish he just called in sick or resigned because he was a distraction to my team. When he went down we had to stop play, wait for the training staff to roll him off the court, and mop the floor before we could continue to play. It was hard to get any sort of flow going those days. When he wasn't there, things were intense and practice was exciting.

I thought I left those antics far behind me when I finished playing basketball, but boy was I wrong. The workplace is a breeding ground for people who consistently get sick and cause a distraction for those who are there to work.

Take some steps to alleviate the problem and keep employees at work instead of home sick. Prevention is the best medicine, open up and say ahhhhh to these healthy ideas:

Take a shot. At education, that is. Have meetings with your employees to help them live right. These meetings usually take place during lunch and feature lively discussions about low-fat cooking, good health practices on the job and CPR training. When it comes to health, you can cover a variety of topics.

Beef up. Promote exercise at the workplace. Some employers put a gym onsite or offer memberships to local workout facilities. It may not take care of all the ailments employees suffer, but it will promote a healthy lifestyle and that is the first step.

Snack time. I often see coworkers slurping down can after can of caffeine-riddled pop while munching on a candy bar or potato chips. As tasty as it sounds, it doesn't take a surgeon general to know it isn't healthy. Replace those traditional vending machines with ones that provide juice, pretzels or other healthy snacks.

Running a successful business takes teamwork. You can't win if your teammates don't show up. Keep 'em healthy and happy and you'll be better for it in the long run.

No one ever got woozy from eating a bagel.

Well, I take that back. My teammate did once. I think someone dropped it on his foot.

Taking a vacation makes a big difference for business owners

The idea of taking time out of a busy schedule to enjoy a vacation is a lot like going to the dentist for some small business owners. I know because I witnessed it first hand. I was at a conference in Florida where small business owners were supposed to gather to iron out national advocacy issues and have some fun in the sun, but what I saw was anything but that.

All of the small business owners took advantage of the chance to discuss national politics, but when it was free time they sprinted to a pay phone, or whipped out their cellular. They checked on the business, the mail, the store, making sure everything was fine. Nobody relaxed. If I didn't know better, I could have sworn I heard a dentist drill in the lobby.

The small business owners complained they were worried their business would fall apart because they weren't there. Some said the people in charge might not be able to do their job, and yet others said it wasn't a good time to leave because of an impending deal.

I refuse to believe that is true. If you can trust your people when you work with them, they won't let you down when you leave. Impending deals know when you are gone and if it's a great deal, it needs to be that way for both parties and they'll wait until you get back.

Here are some ideas to make sure your nerves don't get the best of you when you leave the office and venture out on vacation:

Business and pleasure mix. This one is easy. Like my comrades in Florida, it pays to make sure to do a little of both, so you can not only relax, but also have fun. Continue having your daily fix of stress, but don't dwell on it. Business junkies like this piece of advice best.

Be ready to come back. Work can, and will, pile up while you're gone. The person you left in charge is key to making your return as smooth as possible. Have them scan the mail to make priority lists. Have other key employees present you with updates of what went on while you were gone.

Plan accordingly. Make sure to mark vacation time on a calendar for employees to see well ahead of time. Let them know where you'll be and when you'll be back. Treat it like a project. Timelines work for projects and they do wonders for planning a successful vacation.

These are just a few simple ways to make vacations more enjoyable. It's healthy to worry a bit about being away from your business, but like the going to the dentist, it usually isn't as bad as you think it is.

And quite a bit less painful.

Is your workplace accessible?

I went back to work three days after knee surgery. I simply felt better and couldn't stand being at home another minute. Daytime television was far worse than any pain I could possibly encounter at work. Jerry Springer is quite the motivator.

Armed with my briefcase, medicine, a cooler full of ice for my knee and the demon crutches from Hades, I bravely limped to my office.

A week earlier, trips from my desk to other parts of the office were merely an afterthought, but on my first day back it took me a long time. As the day progressed, I found everything I did took much longer than before. Simple trips to the restroom or drinking fountain were major undertakings. Eating lunch and trekking to the copy room also were tough. Sitting at my desk turned into a constant comfort battle. A battle I often lost.

It's hard being physically challenged, especially in offices unsuited for special needs. I'm lucky. My office was fine and everybody was willing to help. But that isn't always the case.

It's easy to overlook how difficult it might be for a physically challenged person to make their way through your business. A little forethought and planning can make your business accessible and maybe even enjoyable.

Here are some ideas:

Test it out. The best way to see if your business is accessible is to test it out. Get a pair of crutches and "be hurt" for a morning. See what it's like to move around your office. Is your bathroom too far away? Is your drinking fountain too low or too high? Do you have low desks or impossible to reach supplies? Inconveniences you never notice while moving around unrestricted can make a big difference when you're in a wheel chair or huffing and puffing on crutches.

Check the books. Make sure your business complies with any city, state or federal laws. Handicapped stalls, work areas and parking places are just the tip of the iceberg when it comes to making sure your business is accessible.

Be considerate. Do your best to make your workplace open to everyone. Be ready with alternative plans if you have an injured employee or a customer that needs assistance. Make sure your employees know your plans, too.

Knowing the strengths and weaknesses of your office or store's layout can make a big difference in the long run. Imagine how hard it would be to limp along without the support of your customers.

Appendix

What is the Small Business Association of Michigan?

The Small Business Association of Michigan (SBAM) is a statewide trade association organized for the exclusive intent and concern of small business in Michigan. With more than 8,000 members, SBAM is the largest state-based association of small businesses in the nation. It provides leadership in the promotion of free enterprise and other common interests of small businesses in Michigan.

The membership of SBAM is as diverse as Michigan's economy itself. From accounting to appliance stores, vintners to veterinarians, what unites SBAM's membership is the spirit of enterprise. Small business owners start their business because they can do it better, they can do something no one else is doing.

SBAM's primary mission is to help its members succeed by removing the barriers to their success. Those barriers take different forms. Sometimes they are legislative and governmental, sometimes they are economic, sometimes they are educational. Sometimes they are a mixture of all three.

But, whatever form these barriers take, SBAM brings together a network of small business owners to clear away the roadblocks facing small business. All of SBAM's programs and services exist to help small business improve the business climate and conditions in which small business operates.

Who Joins SBAM?

Requirements for joining the Small Business Association of

Michigan are few. A company must have fewer than 500 employees and be a registered business in the state of Michigan.

Nearly all types of businesses are represented — retail, service, professional, construction, agricultural, manufacturing, etc. As a result SBAM members comes from across the spectrum of SIC codes. Gross sales of the typical member range from under $100,000 to under $10 million.

The typical member is concerned about high taxes, finding good employees, government regulations, the cost of employee benefits, decisions made by the state legislature, and controlling costs.

For more information about SBAM, call 800.362.5461.

Visit SBAM on the Web at *www.sbam.org*.